Classrooms in the Factories

CLASSROOMS IN THE FACTORIES

An account of educational activities conducted by American industry

HAROLD F. CLARK *Professor in charge of Educational Economics, Teachers College, Columbia University*

HAROLD S. SLOAN *Director of Research, Fairleigh Dickinson University, Adjunct Professor of Economics, New York University*

INSTITUTE OF RESEARCH

FAIRLEIGH DICKINSON UNIVERSITY · 1958

Distributed by
NEW YORK UNIVERSITY PRESS,
32 Washington Place, New York 3, N.Y.

Library of Congress catalog card number: 58-7833
Manufactured in the United States of America

Intellect and industry are never incompatible. There is more wisdom, and will be more benefit, in combining them than scholars like to believe, or than the common world imagines; life has time enough for both, and its happiness will be increased by the union.

Sharon Turner (1768-1847)

Contents

PREFACE   vii

I   ORIGINS   3

Apprenticeship   4
Corporation Schools   5
Contemporary Education in American Industry   7

II   AN OVERVIEW   13

Educational Activities in General   14
Subject Matter   15
Attendance   16
Multiplant Organizations   17
Industries   17

III   INTEGRATED PROGRAMS   25

Managerial and Supervisory   26
    A Personalized Program   26
    Company Correspondence Courses   29
    Formal Procedure   31
    Personal and Formal   33
    Understudy Training   35
Technical Programs   37
    Keeping Up to Date   37
    Graduate Engineering Program   37
    Developing Assistant Engineers   38
    Making Draftsmen   38

IV   ORIENTATION   41

Orientation for New Factory Workers   41
A Week of Orientation   41
Technical Orientation   43
Engineer Orientation   45

V   A COURSE IN MANAGERIAL AND SUPERVISORY DEVELOPMENT   47

A Course for Supervisors   48

VI   A COURSE IN HUMAN RELATIONS   61

Studying Human Relations   62

Causes of Human Behavior   62
Individual Differences   63
Performance and Abilities   63
Development Through Training   64
Motivation   65
Individual Goals   65
Solving the Problem of Frustration   66
Understanding Workers' Attitudes   68
Counseling   70
Importance of Group Attitudes   72
Communication   73
Leadership Authority   74

VII   TECHNICAL COURSES   77

VIII   GENERAL EDUCATION   83

Consolidated Index of Courses   84

General Programs   97
High-school Courses Included   97
On Company Time   98
A Graded Program   98

Specific Courses   99
Rapid Reading   99
Creative Thinking   103
Economics   107
   Our Dynamic Economy   107
   Inflation   109
   The Business Cycle   111
   Taxation   113
   Federal Spending   116

IX   CO-OPERATION WITH FORMAL EDUCATIONAL INSTITUTIONS   119

College Level, Graduate and Undergraduate   119
Education Below the College Level   123
Scholarships, Fellowships, and Loans   125

X   SOME CONSEQUENCES   127

BIBLIOGRAPHY   136

Preface

This report has to do with the educational activities carried on by leading corporations in American industry. By "education" is here meant a definite program in which knowledge or skills are taught according to some predetermined plan, with periodic group meetings, required assignments and examinations, or some comparable means of judging achievement. All educational programs considered involve formal procedures of this kind. However, they may incorporate informal methods as well, such, for example, as coaching, counseling, field observations, and on-the-job training, the relative weight assigned to formal and informal methods depending upon differing circumstances and policies.

Education which applies exclusively to a particular product or trade, such as sales or apprenticeship training, is not considered. It is to be expected, of course, that most education conducted by industry will be company-oriented to some extent, but there is a wide area between this and the highly restricted sort of subject matter above mentioned. Within this area the report reviews the origin of corporation educational activities, surveys their extent and nature, and analyzes the subject matter with which they deal. Since this is strictly a factual report, no evaluations or criticisms of any kind are presented.

The study is confined to approximately 500 of the largest American industrial corporations, size being measured in terms of dollar sales. For the names of the corporations, the list published in the *Fortune* supplement, July, 1956, was used. Corporate addresses together with the names of educational directors, industrial or public-relations managers, or other officials to whom communications were addressed were taken from *Poor's Register of Directors and Executives,* 1956, and the current supplements of that directory. It is possible, perhaps probable, that the procedures and practices adopted by these largest corporations, the leaders of American industry, are followed fairly closely by American industry in general, at least to the extent that size and resources permit. However this may be, those of the 500 or so largest corporations conducting educational activities of some kind account for a substantial part of the industrial man power of the country. Relevant statistics are shown in Chapter I. Although the number of corporations studied, therefore, constitutes a small proportion of the total number of industrial establishments, the percentage of man power covered is substantial.

Factual material incorporated in the study has been garnered from four sources: (1) questionnaires; (2) personal conferences; (3) brochures, catalogues, announcements, and so forth, distributed by the corporations; and (4) current literature on the subject. Mailed questionnaires invariably present a problem. If too detailed, the response is small; if too general, the information is meaningless. The questionnaire used in this study was aimed somewhere between the two. Questions were so cast that each could be answered by "yes" or "no," and the number of questions was limited to 17. Numerous authorities were consulted in the course of the questionnaire's preparation, and, after agreement as to the contents, it was tested by a sample mailing. The final consensus of opinion was that, although it omitted much that would be helpful to know, it asked about all the information that busy executives could reasonably be expected to supply. Some of the respondents have taken occasion to condemn it, others to commend it, which suggests perhaps that the policy of compromise went not too far astray. A facsimile of the questionnaire together with the two letters that accompanied it will be found in Chapter II.

Every effort was made to reduce the number of nonrespondents to a minimum. An individually typed letter (automatically produced), addressed to the attention of a particular official, accompanied each questionnaire, together with a stamped, addressed, return envelope. A second letter was sent to nonrespondents; in this was enclosed an interim report of the study, in addition to a duplicate questionnaire and another stamped and addressed return envelope. As a result, the response to the questionnaire was unusually large, considering the deluge of such material that constantly descends upon corporation officials.

Even so, the number of nonrespondents presents a problem. It is common knowledge that to apportion answers to them in proportion to those received from the respondents is unjustified, but to ignore the nonrespondents—a method commonly followed —seems no better. The one involves an unjustified assumption on the part of the investigator; the other encourages an unwarranted inference on the part of the reader. If it is said, for example, that from a mailing of 200, 120 answers are received, 30 per cent "yes" and 70 per cent "no," the reader is likely to think of the 30 per cent and 70 per cent as applied to the 200 mailed instead of to the 120 received, and to forget or overlook the 80 unknowns.

In an effort to report the count more realistically therefore, a chart is shown in Chapter II with percentage ranges applied to the entire list of approximately 500. This was compiled by assuming for each "yes" and "no" question, first that all the nonrespondents would have said "yes," then, second, that all the nonrespondents would have said "no." Maximum and minimum percentages were then calculated accordingly. In all probability the extremes in every case are false, but the truth must necessarily be somewhere between the two. Thus, in the above example, the "yes" dispositions are somewhere between 18 and 58 per cent of the total mailing, the spread being accounted for by the 40 per cent unknown. Of course, the higher the percentage of nonrespondents, the wider the spread and the less meaningful the results, but that is as it should be; the percentages reflect what is known, and only to the extent that replies are received is knowledge gained.

Personal conferences have been granted not only willingly but with gracious hospitality and a most generous expenditure of both time and effort. In only one instance was one refused. Indeed, they might have continued with profit almost indefinitely, except for the restricted time free from academic duties available to the authors. For the privilege of meeting so many corporation executives, discovering the wealth of ideas and ideals held in common, sensing the dedication they hold to the tasks they pursue, and witnessing at first hand the emphasis so often placed upon developing effective citizenship and understanding minds as well as business efficiency and technical competence, the authors are profoundly thankful. To them, these conferences were indeed a rich educational experience.

For time and knowledge so unsparingly given in response to special requests, particular thanks are due the American Telephone and Telegraph Company, the Bendix Aviation Corp., the Curtiss-Wright Corporation, the Flintkote Co., the Ford Motor Company, the General Electric Company, the International Business Machines Corporation, Johnson & Johnson, the Socony Mobil Oil Company, Inc., the Union Bag-Camp Paper Corporation, and the Western Electric Company, Inc. Thanks are due also to the hundreds of officials who took the trouble to answer the questionnaire, and by so doing made this report possible. And we are grateful to the score or more who, by amplifying it through subsequent correspondence, added much to our knowledge.

For informal corporation publications, the files of the office of the Industrial Co-ordinator at Fairleigh Dickinson University were made available. The collection proved unusually comprehensive, conveniently accessible, and most helpful in supplementing personal conferences. Numerous examples have been drawn from this literature, credit being accorded when the corporations concerned have expressly given their consent. Otherwise, the understanding that no proper names would be mentioned has been carefully followed.

Other literature bearing specifically on the subject appears fragmentary; many references appear in more general business publications, however, and will be found in footnotes throughout the report as well as in the bibliography.

The report proceeds from general observations to more specific discussions. Chapter I reviews the origin of the movement for education in industry. Chapter II reports on the returns from the questionnaire. Chapter III describes a number of integrated educational programs in managerial development and technical instruction. Chapters IV to VIII, inclusive, explain in detail subject matter and teaching methods used in various courses included within the five general areas specified in the questionnaire. Chapter IX considers various policies for co-operating with formal educational institutions. Chapter X discusses the impact of education in industry upon American civilization as a whole.

All the information contained in this report has come directly or indirectly from industry. Corporation personnel, therefore, will probably find in it little that is new. To them, however, it may be of interest to see an over-all picture of industry's activities in education and to view their own programs in the light of this background. Those less familiar with industry will be interested, it is believed, to learn of this dynamic and rapidly developing sector of education and to judge its significance to American culture. Certainly, to those whose careers started a generation or so ago, the educational opportunities currently offered by industry in preparation for, and, increasingly, as a necessary continuing activity in so many vocations of absorbing interest, will, perhaps, appear little short of astounding.

New York, 1957   H. F. C. and H. S. S.

Classrooms in the Factories

1 Origins

Factories today have classrooms, organized programs of studies, faculties, textbooks and examinations, and even graduation exercises with diplomas. Educational budgets often rival those of good-sized colleges,[1] and expenditures per student are not infrequently two and a half or three times the national average for conventional institutions.[2]

The classrooms are often superbly equipped with the latest model blackboards, projectors, and sound recording devices. Sometimes movable partitions, on ceiling tracks, permit a group of classrooms to be combined into a moderate-sized auditorium. The courses of study range all the way from subjects having to do with a particular product to those of a more general nature dealing with business, technical, and even cultural matters. The faculty may consist of full- or part-time instructors, drawn from the company staff, professors borrowed from some nearby or even distant university, or a combination of all three. Indeed, it can be said without exaggeration that a new sector is being added to the traditional pattern of American public and private education.

Not all factories, of course, provide such facilities, but they are

[1] William H. Whyte, Jr., *The Organization Man,* Simon and Schuster, Inc., New York, 1956, p. 120.

[2] The average institutional expenditure per student for a 4-year course in American universities and colleges is approximately $4,000. (*Statistical Abstract of the United States,* 77th Ann. ed., U.S. Department of Commerce, Washington, D.C., 1956, p. 125.) Corporation expenditures per student of $10,000 and $12,000 were reported in conferences with corporation educational directors.

found to a greater or lesser extent in a predominant number of America's largest corporations and are available, under varying conditions, to a large percentage of the nation's industrial workers.[3]

How did this all come about, and what is the motivating force behind it? To be sure, American industry has conducted educational programs of a kind from the very beginning of manufacturing on this continent, but never to an extent such as now, with programs comprehending such a wide range of subject matter, and classes attended by corporation personnel from the humblest filing clerk to the top executive.

Apprenticeship

Probably all education within industry began with the institution of apprenticeship. The indenture, signed in 1718, which bound Benjamin Franklin to his brother for a term of 9 years to learn the printing trade, was typical of many. Obligations incurred by the masters were few and vague; regulations imposed upon the trainee were many and rigid, with little compensation other than board, lodging, and clothing. Even the famous Franklin did not endure the hardships and injustices long enough to "graduate," and there was little improvement in the procedure during his lifetime. Then, with the factory system, firmly established in the United States by 1850, this so-called domestic type of apprenticeship soon came to an end. Money wages gradually replaced compensation in kind, and by 1865 a system of graduated wages based on period of employment had appeared. But otherwise the status of apprentices was slow to change. Even during the 1880's, in many cases, a boy's parents had to compensate the industrialist for the expenses incurred in the course of training,

[3] Total employment in mining and manufacturing (June, 1955) was 16,477,000. (*Handbook of Basic Economic Statistics,* Economic Statistics Bureau of Washington, D.C., January, 1957, p. 17.) Total employment (1955) in 296 of the largest (measured in terms of sales) American industrial corporations responding to a questionnaire and reporting educational activities of some kind was 6,391,717. The total employment in nonrespondent corporations was 1,872,351. If all the nonrespondents have educational activities of some kind, the percentage would be 50.1; if none of them have, the percentage would be 38.7.

and, as late as 1913, the wages paid were little better than those before the turn of the century.[4]

Government intervention changed all of this. In 1915 the state of Wisconsin pioneered with legislation providing for an organized system of modern apprenticeship, and 22 years later the federal government followed with the Fitzgerald Act,[5] the essential provisions of which remain to this day (1957). National standards of instruction, wages, supervision, and evaluation are determined by a federal policy-making body; administration is cared for by a division within the Department of Labor, and some 7,000 local committees supervise the various apprenticeship programs currently carried on within their respective territories.[6] As a result, apprenticeship programs are today contributing liberally to the need for both skilled workers and supervisory talent. Each year approximately 70,000 graduates enter the skilled-labor force, and, although this number contributes only 28 per cent of the 250,000 necessary to replace annual losses through death, transfer, and retirement, it constitutes a particularly well-trained group, many of whom, with supplementary education, can be upgraded into positions of greater responsibility.[7] A recent (1954) survey of construction companies shows that 173 top officials and 353 managers, superintendents, and foremen had started as apprentices. Another study of a large electrical and automotive equipment concern reveals that 120 of the 300 apprenticed graduates who were employed by the company at the time the study was made held important supervisory and managerial positions.[8]

Corporation Schools

But long before the modernization of apprenticeship systems

[4] *Apprenticeship Past and Present,* 3rd ed., U.S. Department of Labor, Bureau of Apprenticeship, Washington, D.C., 1955, *passim.*

[5] Public—No. 308—75th Congress, Chap. 663, 1st Session H. R. 7274.

[6] William Patterson and Marion Hedges, *Educating for Industry Through Apprenticeship,* Prentice-Hall, Inc., Englewood Cliffs, N.J., 1947, pp. 15, 16.

[7] *Business Week,* McGraw-Hill Publishing Company, Inc., New York, Aug. 18, 1956, p. 64.

[8] *Apprenticeship Past and Present,* 3rd ed., U.S. Department of Labor, Bureau of Apprenticeship, Washington, D.C., 1955, pp. 29, 30.

through state and federal legislation, American manufacturers had taken upon themselves the task of providing more comprehensive educational programs. Indeed, they had been forced to do so. The striking expansion of the economy after the middle of the nineteenth century, with its insistent demand for skilled labor, and the fact that in the United States, even by 1870, no public or private educational institution on a secondary level offered industrial training, left the industrialists little choice but to establish their own schools.[9] Accordingly, the corporation school came into existence. At least five such schools were established between 1872 and 1901, and from that time on their numbers increased rapidly. By 1916, it is estimated that some 60,000 boys were attending such schools, and the National Association of Corporation Schools, organized in 1913, is reported to have had 150 members when it merged with the American Management Association in 1922.[10]

Corporation schools operated according to no set pattern. In most cases, students were selected, and their training consisted of areas of study ranging all the way from the more technical aspects of production to many subjects taught in the public schools. Some were full-time classroom schools; others combined the classroom with factory and office work. A few companies made it possible for any employee to attend classes in outside institutions while carrying on part-time work with the company. These were classes in advertising, selling and distribution, business education, English for foreigners, and in more specialized areas applicable to a particular product. One appraisal, comparing the corporation schools with the regular public schools, found the former superior in responsiveness of students, recitation technique, and mental discipline; the latter superior in teaching, breadth of view, and general cultural development. In large measure, however, the corporation schools attained their objectives. Business training paved the way for many promotions, the

[9] U.S. Commissioner of Labor, *17th Annual Report,* Washington, D.C., 1902, p. 20.

[10] This account of corporation schools is drawn largely from A. J. Beatty, *Corporation Schools,* Public School Publishing Company, Bloomington, Ill., 1918.

quality of production improved, and labor turnover was better controlled, while waste and the number of accidents were reduced.

Contemporary Education in American Industry

During the early days of the present century, apprenticeship training, supplemented by the corporation schools, together with practical on-the-job experience, were considered the most effective preparation for a career in industry. Anything in the nature of very much book knowledge was regarded as superfluous if not a handicap. The liberal-arts degree was looked upon with indifference, if not outright hostility.[11] Henry Ford's famous dictum, "It is one to me, if a man comes from Sing Sing or Harvard," was perhaps typical of the more tolerant attitude.[12]

Nevertheless, with the constantly increasing size and complexity of industrial organizations, problems mounted.[13] In 1921 the American Federated Engineering Societies, after investigating efficiency in certain areas of production, reported that from 50 to 75 per cent of the waste was due to ineffective management.[14] Indeed, the scarcity of managerial talent had already been felt keenly during the World War I period. At the outset of hostilities, there existed some 20 per cent over-all surplus capacity in American factories.[15] This was quickly absorbed by the influx of munitions orders. Vestibule schools, consisting of machines set up apart from the regular production operations, were hastily organized to teach quickly the skills necessary for certain specialized operations. But managerial talent, it was discovered, could not be so easily acquired, and the industrialists began to look to the colleges and universities for relief.

[11] Mabel Newcomer, *The Big Business Executive, the Factors That Made Him,* Columbia University Press, New York, 1955, p. 66.

[12] Sigmund Diamond, *The Reputation of the American Businessman,* Harvard University Press, Cambridge, Mass., 1955, p. 157.

[13] *The Executive Life,* The Editors of Fortune, Doubleday & Company, Inc., New York, 1956, p. 135.

[14] *The Encyclopaedia of the Social Sciences,* The Macmillan Company, New York, 1930, Vol. 10, p. 79.

[15] Harold Moulton, *Income and Economic Progress,* Brookings Institution, Washington, D.C., 1935, pp. 17-21.

For a time it seemed that the formal educational institutions might fill the gap. Before the turn of the century, only 3 universities offered business training. Within three decades the number had increased to between 180 and 200. In 1915 the enrollment was about 9,000; in 1930 it was 60,000.[16] In 1955 first-level degrees in business and commerce were conferred upon 41,000 graduates, more than in any other field of study with the single exception of education.[17]

Industry accepted these graduates, not without complaint regarding the difficulties encountered in bridging the gap between academic and business life; little was done, however, to resolve the problem. More compelling reasons had to be forthcoming before industrialists, in any great number, determined to supplement academic training with adequate, modern educational programs of their own. As late as 1946, the National Industrial Conference Board observed that only slightly over 5 per cent of 3,459 respondents reported having an executive-training program.[18]

But events soon conspired to bring these compelling reasons to the fore. The depression of the 1930's reduced business activity to a trickle. Social security, legislated in 1935, and the increasing number of private pension plans, established during the following decade,[19] encouraged early retirements. Furthermore World War II took its toll in man power just at a time when colossal demands were being made upon industry, and new processes, designed to speed up production, were being adopted increasingly in factory operations. In consequence, problems of organizational integration and technical adjustment increased in number and complexity. And they have, in fact, continued to this day, for the postwar adjustment brought no recession, as many had predicted. Indeed, World War II may be said to have ushered in what future historians may well term a second industrial revolution,

[16] *The Encyclopaedia of the Social Sciences,* The Macmillan Company, New York, 1930, Vol. 3, p. 109.

[17] *Statistical Abstract of the United States,* 77th Ann. ed., U.S. Department of Commerce, Washington, D.C., 1956, p. 13L.

[18] *Studies in Personnel Policy No. 107,* National Industrial Conference Board, New York, p. 3.

[19] *Special Report No. 44,* National Policy Association, Washington, D.C., 1956, p. 7.

overlapping the first and destined, perhaps, to cause even more far-reaching changes in the economic life of the nation.[20]

It is these changes in process and prospect that are responsible for the great upsurge of education in industry today. Product diversification, multiplant development, and decentralized organization necessitate a prolonged period of induction and suitable orientation procedures for new recruits; man-power shortage calls for upgrading and retraining on a huge scale; and, above all, new techniques of management, the never-ending streams of new inventions flowing from the experimental laboratories and research centers, and the rapidly progressing plans for atomic energy and automation require that corporation personnel be continuously informed and instructed and remain flexible, ever receptive to change. The notion that education ends with a college degree is completely untenable in industry today. Colleges and universities are doing what they can to provide basic technical, managerial, and liberal-arts training as well as specialized instruction in graduate programs, seminars, and institutes, but the pace is so rapid that educational institutions removed even one step from the reality of production are frequently lacking in both equipment and experience.[21] Just as the center of research, during recent years, seems to have shifted from the universities to industry, so the trend in this more functional type of education appears to be in the same direction.[22]

The immediate objective is utility, whether it be the most effec-

[20] E. M. Hugh-Jones (ed.), *The Push-Button World, Automation Today,* University of Oklahoma Press, Norman, Okla., 1956, p. 125.

[21] *Instrumentation and Automation,* Hearings before the Subcommittee on Economic Stabilization of the Joint Economic Committee, Congress of the United States, Second Session, Dec. 12, 13, and 14, 1956, U.S. Government Printing Office, Washington, D.C., 1957, p. 12.

[22] While funds devoted to research and development increased from about 1½ to 5 billion dollars from 1945 to 1955 the amount from government sources decreased from 70 per cent to 50 per cent; the amount from universities remained at a constant 2 per cent; the percentage from industry increased from 28 to 48. Funds used by government decreased from 28 per cent to 19 per cent; funds used by universities increased 1 per cent with considerable fluctuations during the 10-year period; funds used by industry increased fairly steadily from 65 per cent to 73 per cent. (*Statistical Abstract of the United States,* 77th Ann. ed., U.S. Department of Commerce, Washington, D.C., 1956, p. 499.)

tive methods of selling, the most approved processes of production, or just getting along with co-workers. But often there is idealism too, and a profound belief in education as a way of life. Even the most rigid company orientation may carry the trainee far beyond the limits of knowledge immediately applicable to a given product or policy. Mathematics is a prerequisite for handling business machines in almost any capacity; a study of petroleum can hardly escape beginning somewhere within the area of economic geography, and certainly anything learned about human relations is applicable far beyond the confines of a single organization. Nevertheless, these broader concepts are usually by-products—not ends in themselves.

The motive is nothing short of a life career in some absorbing creative activity, with constant shifts and changes to challenge the imagination. To that end the trainees work at their preparation longer hours, more intensively, and more purposefully than they did at their college tasks. "Now we are playing for keeps," they say, and mean it. Nor do they become submerged in any common reservoir of impersonal relationships. Sometimes a whole staff of teachers, supervisors, and counselors is at hand to instruct, encourage, and advise as well as to evaluate each trainee's current progress and potential possibilities. The new industrial revolution, if such there be, has shifted the focus of attention from production to man, and the reason is clear.[23] When human beings are properly prepared and motivated, productivity need cause little worry.[24]

Many of those who have reached the top echelons would like to see this specialized training superimposed upon a broad liberal education.[25] As they see it, business problems today demand an understanding of history, literature, and philosophy quite as much as technology and management.[26] In fact, the nearer the

[23] Mason Haire, *Psychology in Management,* McGraw-Hill Book Company, Inc., New York, 1956, p. 48.

[24] Edward C. Bursk (ed.), *Human Relations for Management, the Newer Perspective,* Harper & Brothers, New York, 1956, pp. 27, 34.

[25] Mable Newcomer, *op. cit.,* p. 66.

[26] W. Lloyd Warner and James C. Abegglen, *Big Business Leaders in America,* Harper & Brothers, New York, 1955, p. 47, 48.

top, the more general the education required.[27] Training directors
frequently express similar sentiments. They point out that corporations that have accepted recruits with engineering or business
degrees sometimes find it desirable to send them back to college
for exposure to the liberal arts and humanities before placing
them in high posts, thus necessitating a time-consuming interruption in their careers.[28] It is a question whether those who do
the actual recruiting among the colleges and universities carry
out these injunctions;[29] maybe specialized degrees offer a tempt-
ing immediate short cut to the current pressure to fill openings.
However this may be, a sizable percentage of business executives
in leading American corporations today have started their careers
with liberal-arts training and evidently feel that this background
makes for more effective management.[30]

Thus has education come into its own, not only as a pre-

[27] Gilbert W. Chapman, "Educating Tomorrow's Executives," *The Management Review,* American Management Association, New York, March,
1957, p. 78.

[28] William H. Whyte, Jr., *op. cit.,* p. 101.

[29] *Ibid.,* p. 102.

[30] "A study (1953) of the educational training of 2,175 principals (officers
and partners) in a random 25 per cent sample of 3,784 business organizations listed in *Who's Who in Commerce and Industry,* Vol. 7, A. N. Mar-
quis Co., Chicago, Illinois, 1951, concludes that:

"1. It can be said at the 99 per cent level of confidence that there are
between 5.7 and 7.4 chances out of 10 that the principal is a college graduate. The younger the principal, the greater the chances. (Coefficient of correlation .91.)

"2. If the principal is a college graduate it can be said at the 99 per cent level
of confidence that there are between 5.6 and 7.9 chances out of ten that his
formal education was of a nontechnical nature (liberal arts, law, or business). The younger the principal the greater the chances. (Coefficient of
correlation .32.)

"3. If the principal was a nontechnical graduate it can be said at the 99 per
cent level of confidence that the chances are between 6.2 and 7.1 out of
10 that he holds an A.B.; Ph.B.; B.S. in liberal arts, or some comparable
degree in liberal arts; that the chances are between 2.1 and 2.8 out of 10
that he holds a LL.B.; that the chances are between 0.7 and 1.2 out of 10
that he holds some degree in business." Harold S. Sloan, "The Educational
Backgrounds of Business Leaders in the United States," *Challenge Magazine,*
Institute of Economic Affairs, New York University, New York, December,
1953.

See also Warner and Abegglen, *op. cit.,* p. 48.

requisite to an industrial career, but as a continuous adjunct to it.[31] To suggest that what industry is teaching transcends in importance what it is producing seems fantastic in view of the mechanical wonders about which so much is being said, but education itself is a powerful tool; it is probably the most powerful tool that mankind has yet devised for molding the kind of civilization that is wanted.[32] This new and rapidly expanding sector of American education, therefore, is capable of engendering change quite as far reaching, and probably much more fundamental, than all the ingenious things pouring off the assembly lines.

How extensive it is, what is being taught, and the possible consequences are told in the following pages.

[31] Mable Newcomer, *op. cit.*, p. 146.
[32] Eugene Staley (Ed.), *Creating an Industrial Civilization, a Report on the Corning Conference,* Harper & Brothers, New York, 1952, p. 37.

A predominant number of large industrial corporations today conduct educational programs of some kind. Industry apparently believes that no longer can mere chance be relied upon for the discovery of leadership talent. Such ability, it is said, too frequently does not manifest itself automatically but may lie dormant for no better reason than the common human failure to develop innate capacity to its full stature. Executives point out that, even if the percentage of such underdeveloped leadership qualities in any one corporation is small, what exists is precious, and what remains undiscovered is waste, just as surely as though it appeared as an unnecessary expense item in the balance sheet. Of course, personal development must of necessity be self-development, but motivation is often necessary, encouragement can speed up the process, and periodic evaluation can provide a continuing stimulus. Industry is supplying these aids through planned, systematic educational programs, some extensive, others less so, but all with the common objective of making personal development a continuous life process. The present chapter presents an overview of this movement—its extent, its nature, and the personnel who take part in it.

The information comes from a questionnaire directed to 482 of the largest American industrial corporations,[1] a facsimile of

---

[1] For an explanation of the questionnaire, its preparation, and so forth, see pp. x and xi of the preface. Holding companies, mergers, and other items held ineligible account for the 18 deletions from the source list of 500.

which is shown on page 21; a copy of the letter that accompanied it appears on page 19. One follow-up letter, sent to those who failed to respond to the first, is shown on page 20. Together, these brought 349 replies, or 72.4 per cent of the total mailing. The complete count is shown on page 22.

Educational Activities in General

Of those replying to the questionnaire, 296, or 84.8 per cent, reported carrying on some sort of educational activity requiring regular attendance by the participants. Even if the 133 who did not reply carry on no such activities, the percentage of the 482 corporations queried would be 61.4, and if all the nonrespondents could answer affirmatively, the percentage would be 89.0. No doubt both extremes are highly unlikely, but, assuming only the accuracy of the answers, the actual percentage must be somewhere in between.[2]

Most of the corporations (66.8 per cent of those reporting educational activities) conduct a program entirely within the jurisdiction of the corporation as well as one carried on outside of its jurisdiction in one or more colleges or universities. Some report only the former (84, or 28.3 per cent), and a very few report only the latter (5, or 1.6 per cent). Of the total number of 482 corporations, it can be said that between 41.0 and 70.5 per cent offer educational activities both within and without the corporation; between 17.4 and 46.8 per cent offer only the first, and between 1.0 and 30.4 per cent, only the second.

All of the corporations reporting educational activities of their own stated that the teaching staff consisted of their regular personnel acting in that capacity either full or part time. About half (49.6 per cent) reported supplementing their own teaching staff with college professors or others of comparable authority engaged on a part-time basis, between 29.0 and 58.5 per cent of the total mailing falling within this category.

Almost all of the corporations offering their employees educational opportunities in colleges or universities reported defraying the expenses in whole or in part (198, or 97.5 per cent). Many

[2] For an explanation of the computation, see p. xi of the preface.

explanatory notes on the questionnaires pointed out that this policy was contingent upon grades received, high grades bringing greater assistance in some cases. Only 5, or 2.4 per cent, replied negatively to this query regarding expense. It can be said, then, that between 41.0 and 70.5 per cent of the 482 corporations defray a part or all of the expenses of employees taking courses in colleges and universities.

Subject Matter

Five divisions of subject matter were mentioned in the questionnaire. It should not be inferred, however, that because they are thus stated separately, they are necessarily taught separately. In many cases they are. On the other hand, an orientation program for new employees may well include a certain amount of subject matter in all five divisions; a managerial development program would, in all probability, include some aspects of human relations; and even a program comprised mainly of technical and professional subjects might conceivably include managerial material as well. Whether taught separately or not, however, the questionnaires indicate that if a company has any educational program at all, it probably includes as many as three or more of the subject-matter divisions mentioned. In 12.5 per cent of the returns from the 296 corporations carrying on educational activities, all subject-matter divisions were checked affirmatively; in 45.2 per cent, all were checked affirmatively with the exception of general education; and in 14.1 per cent, all were checked affirmatively with the exception of general education and technical and professional. These account for 71.8 per cent of the returns. The remaining 28.2 per cent presented a variety of combinations,[3] but none with a frequency of over 3 per cent. In any case, this part of the questionnaire depicts only the general area of subject matter treated, not its depth in any particular category, this latter problem being reserved for later discussion.[4]

Considered individually, orientation and managerial development programs are the most common, being conducted by 93.2

[3] "Yes" and "no" as well as no answer.
[4] See Chaps. IV to VIII, inclusive.

and 90.5 per cent, respectively, of those carrying on educational activities. Human relations ranks third, with 85.4 per cent; technical and professional, fourth, with 67.9 per cent, and general education appears last, with 15.8 per cent. Of the total mailing, it can be said that between 57.2 and 86.0 per cent offer instruction in orientation, between 55.6 and 84.6 per cent teach managerial and supervisory development, between 52.2 and 81.5 per cent include human relations, between 41.7 and 73.2 per cent offer technical and professional subjects, and between 9.7 and 44.8 per cent offer general education.

Attendance

In the matter of attendance, no dominant groupings appear, educational opportunities being offered the various classifications of employees in almost every possible combination. Foremen and supervisors participate most frequently, the percentage being 92.5 of the returns from all corporations reporting educational programs. Junior executives rank next at 77.7 per cent; the business and professional group comes third with 70.6 per cent. A sharp drop appears in the next group, senior executives participating in 53.7 per cent of the corporations.

In the course of personal interviews, it was pointed out that status forbids a senior executive from regular participation in a class conducted by a subordinate. This is understandable. At the same time, many educational directors insist that education in industry must infiltrate the organization from the top down.[5]

This gap is filled, in large part, by attendance at the various conferences organized and conducted by the American Management Association and other similar organizations, as well as by many of the colleges and universities. The 1957-1958 *Seminar Catalogue* of the A.M.A. lists over 200 workshop and orientation seminars offered during the period from September, 1957, through January, 1958, and estimates that over 80,000 executives will attend its conferences, courses, clinics, and related activities during the year. The National Industrial Conference Board lists 29 executive

[5] Douglas H. Fryer, Mortimer R. Feinberg, and Sheldon S. Zalkind, *Developing People in Industry*, Harper & Brothers, New York, 1956, p. 27.

management courses offered by universities, ranging in duration from 3 to 23 weeks.[6]

Courses are offered factory operatives in 44.5 per cent of the companies. Less than a third (31.4 per cent) reported having educational programs available to the clerical staff, and a negligible 3 per cent offer instruction to the families of personnel. The "no" answers make a spread in percentages applicable to the total mailing progressively wider as the list is read from the top down. Of the entire mailing of 482, it may be said that between 56.8 and 86.0 per cent offer instruction to foremen and supervisors; between 47.7 and 78.2 per cent to junior executives; between 43.3 and 76.7 per cent to business professionals; between 32.9 and 66.8 per cent to senior executives; between 27.3 and 62.2 per cent to factory operatives; between 19.2 and 55.6 per cent to the clerical staff; and between 1.8 and 39.8 per cent to the families of corporation employees.

Multiplant Organizations

It should be noted that many of the 482 largest industrial corporations are multiplant organizations with considerable autonomy permitted the educational directors in the various plants. In every case, however, the questionnaire was sent to the company headquarters, and those that were returned came from that source. Many of the returned questionnaires were accompanied by explanations pointing out that operations varied in different plants according to local circumstances and demands, and that the answers indicated on the questionnaire represented the corporation's over-all policy rather than a uniform procedure in all locations. Subsequent personal interviews disclosed that, while practices do vary among the various units in multiplant organizations, the general comprehensive reports gave a fair approximation of the educational activities offered.

Industries

The questionnaire discloses no correlation between particular

[6] *Highlights for the Executive, Studies in Personnel Policy No. 160,* National Industrial Conference Board, New York.

industries and interest in or lack of interest in educational programs. The 53 corporations reporting no such activities represent 27 different industries.[7] Industrial classification is difficult because of the wide product diversification characteristic of so many of the 482 corporations considered in this study, but it would seem that the 27 industries represented by the corporations not carrying on educational activities are also represented by many corporations which do. The questionnaires give no significant clue, therefore, as to the reasons for the absence of educational activities in the 53 corporations thus reporting. A few questionnaires were accompanied by covering letters expressing particular interest in this study and explaining that educational programs were just in the process of organization in their plants. Maybe some companies have just not got around to it.

[7] The *Classified Index of Occupations and Industries of 1950 Census of Population* was used; U.S. Department of Commerce, Bureau of the Census, Washington, D.C., 1950.

EDUCATIONAL ACTIVITIES CONDUCTED BY UNITED STATES INDUSTRY . . . . A SURVEY.

HAROLD F. CLARK   Professor in charge of Educational Economics.
Teachers College. Columbia University.
HAROLD S. SLOAN   Adjunct Professor of Economics.
New York University.

September 10, 1956

. . . .
. . . .
. . . .

Dear Mr. . . . .

Many business executives as well as educators want to know about educational training programs apparently being offered increasingly by American industry. We are endeavoring to gather information on this subject and to that end seek your assistance. You will, of course, receive the results of our findings in due course.

If you feel justified in helping to make this study possible, will you kindly check the simple "yes" or "no" questions stated on the accompanying sheet and return it in the enclosed stamped and addressed envelope.

This study has only to do with the extent and kind of training being offered; we have no intention of trying to evaluate the results of such training. No proper names of corporations or individuals will be mentioned in any reports resulting from this survey.[8]

Respectfully yours,

Adjunct Professor of Economics
Graduate School of Arts and Science
New York University.

---

[8] Where corporate names are mentioned in this report, special permission has been granted to use them, or else they appear in formal publications the titles to which are given.

EDUCATIONAL ACTIVITIES CONDUCTED BY UNITED STATES INDUSTRY . . . . A SURVEY.

HAROLD F. CLARK Professor in charge of Educational Economics.
Teachers College. Columbia University.
HAROLD S. SLOAN Adjunct Professor of Economics.
New York University.

January 7, 1957

. . . .
. . . .
. . . .

Dear Mr. . . . .

You may be interested in the enclosed tabulation showing the replies received thus far from 256 of the 500 largest industrial corporations regarding their educational activities.

We are in hopes that you may feel disposed to cooperate in this survey by returning the accompanying questionnaire. Only a few check marks are required, and a stamped and addressed envelope is enclosed for your convenience.

No corporate or individual names will be mentioned in any publication resulting from this study, and you will, of course, receive a copy of the final report which we believe will prove an interesting document.

Sincerely yours,

Adjunct Professor of Economics
Graduate School of Arts and Science
New York University.

EDUCATIONAL ACTIVITIES CONDUCTED BY UNITED STATES INDUSTRY — A SURVEY

Just check-

CORPORATION TRAINING ACTIVITIES

ON-THE-JOB TRAINING

Training in one or more semi-skilled operations confined to the needs of a particular job, conducted on the job site or in vestibule schools

OFF-THE-JOB TRAINING

Training in general attitudes, administration, technical knowledge, or cultural subjects; conducted by formal educational institutions or by the corporation using its own personnel or professional instructors.

	DO YOU CONDUCT TRAINING IN ANY OF THESE AREAS?
ORIENTATION Knowledge of company regulations and policies; familiarity with authority and responsibility assigned to workers: creation of attitudes of confidence, pride in product, etc.	YES ☐ NO ☐
MANAGERIAL AND SUPERVISORY Techniques concerned with organizing, planning, directing, controlling, and other subjects falling within the scope of scientific management.	YES ☐ NO ☐
TECHNICAL AND PROFESSIONAL Engineering, chemistry, physics, and other specialized subjects relating to the company's activities; training in research for younger personnel.	YES ☐ NO ☐
HUMAN RELATIONS Principles of human behavior; methods for joint problem solving; techniques of communication; understanding individual attitudes and personalities.	YES ☐ NO ☐
GENERAL EDUCATION Current events; popular psychology; languages and other cultural interests.	YES ☐ NO ☐

OTHER AREAS OF OFF-THE-JOB TRAINING NOT SPECIFIED ABOVE

IS ANY OF THIS TRAINING CONDUCTED BY FORMAL EDUCATIONAL INSTITUTIONS SUCH AS SCHOOLS AND COLLEGES?	YES ☐ NO ☐
AT COMPANY EXPENSE?	YES ☐ NO ☐
IS ANY OF THIS TRAINING CONDUCTED DIRECTLY BY THE CORPORATION; THAT IS USING COMPANY PERSONNEL AS INSTRUCTORS	YES ☐ NO ☐
ARE THE COMPANY INSTRUCTORS RESPONSIBLE FOR DUTIES OTHER THAN INSTRUCTION	YES ☐ NO ☐
ARE COLLEGE PROFESSORS OR OTHER SPECIALISTS EMPLOYED AS INSTRUCTORS ON A PART-TIME BASIS BY THE CORPORATION?	YES ☐ NO ☐
ARE CLASSES OR GROUP MEETINGS ATTENDED REGULARLY BY:	
FACTORY OPERATIVES?	YES ☐ NO ☐
FOREMEN, SUPERVISORS?	YES ☐ NO ☐
BUSINESS PROFESSIONALS (ENGINEERS, CHEMISTS, ETC.)?	YES ☐ NO ☐
CLERICAL STAFF?	YES ☐ NO ☐
JUNIOR EXECUTIVES?	YES ☐ NO ☐
SENIOR EXECUTIVES?	YES ☐ NO ☐
FAMILIES OF EMPLOYEES?	YES ☐ NO ☐

Questions answered by:

_____

Date _____

Comments, criticisms and suggestions are welcome. Use the reverse side of this sheet if desired.

Please return this sheet in the accompanying stamped and addressed envelope to:

Dr. Harold F. Clark
Teachers College, Columbia University
New York 27, New York

RESULTS OF QUESTIONNAIRE—ACTUAL COUNT

Area of this survey, 500 largest (measured by sales) American industrial corporations. List published by Fortune (supplement, July, 1956). Deductions for holding companies, mergers, and other items held ineligible, 18. Total mailing, original and one follow-up, 482.

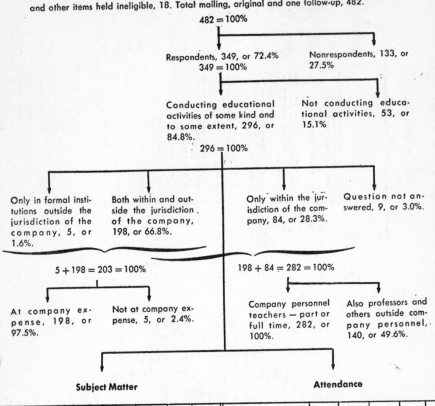

482 = 100%

Respondents, 349, or 72.4%
349 = 100%

Nonrespondents, 133, or 27.5%

Conducting educational activities of some kind and to some extent, 296, or 84.8%.

Not conducting educational activities, 53, or 15.1%

296 = 100%

Only in formal institutions outside the jurisdiction of the company, 5, or 1.6%.

Both within and outside the jurisdiction of the company, 198, or 66.8%.

Only within the jurisdiction of the company, 84, or 28.3%.

Question not answered, 9, or 3.0%.

5 + 198 = 203 = 100%

At company expense, 198, or 97.5%.

Not at company expense, 5, or 2.4%.

198 + 84 = 282 = 100%

Company personnel teachers — part or full time, 282, or 100%.

Also professors and others outside company personnel, 140, or 49.6%.

Subject Matter

Subject Matter	Offered	Per Cent	Not Offered	No Answer	Total
Orientation	276	93.2	14	6	296
Managerial and Supervisory	268	90.5	21	7	296
Human Relations	253	85.4	36	7	296
Technical and Professional	201	67.9	76	19	296
General Education	47	15.8	213	36	296

Attendance

Personnel	Attend	Per Cent	Do Not Attend	No Answer	Total
Foremen and Supervisors	274	92.5	14	8	29
Junior Executives	230	77.7	52	14	29
Business Professionals	209	70.6	59	28	29
Senior Executives	159	53.7	107	30	29
Factory Operatives	132	44.5	129	35	29
Clerical Staff	93	31.4	161	42	29
Families of Personnel	9	3.0	237	50	29

RESULTS OF QUESTIONNAIRE IN TERMS OF TOTAL MAILING

OF THE 482 LARGEST AMERICAN INDUSTRIAL CORPORATIONS, IT CAN BE SAID:

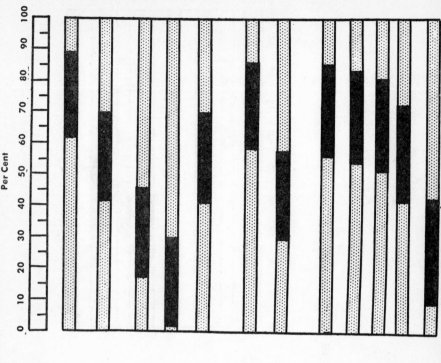

Per Cent

A. IN REGARD EDUCATIONAL ACTIVITIES IN GENERAL, THAT:

1. between 61.4 and 89.0 per cent offer educational activities of some kind and to some extent.

2. between 41.0 and 70.5 per cent offer these activities both within the jurisdiction of the corporation and outside its jurisdiction in formal educational institutions.

3. between 17.4 and 46.8 per cent offer these activities only within the jurisdiction of the corporation.

4. between 1.0 and 30.4 per cent offer these activities only in formal educational institutions.

5. between 41.0 and 70.5 per cent assume the expenses of education in outside institutions either in whole or in part.

B. IN REGARD TEACHING STAFF, THAT:

1. between 58.5 and 87.9 per cent use their own personnel either part or full time.

2. between 29.0 and 58.5 per cent employ college professors or other authorities other than their own personnel on a part-time basis.

C. IN REGARD SUBJECT MATTER, THAT:

1. between 57.2 and 86.0 per cent offer instruction in orientation.

2. between 55.6 and 84.6 per cent offer instruction in managerial and supervisory development.

3. between 52.2 and 81.5 per cent offer instruction in human relations.

4. between 41.7 and 73.2 per cent offer instruction in technical and professional subjects.

5. between 9.7 and 44.8 per cent offer instruction in general educational subjects.

RESULTS OF QUESTIONNAIRE IN TERMS OF TOTAL MAILING (CONTINUED)

Per Cent

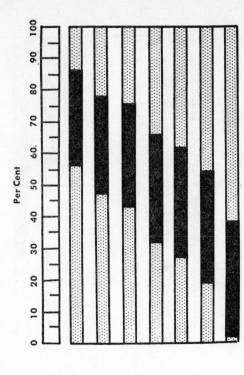

D. IN REGARD THOSE TO WHOM THE INSTRUCTION IS OFFERED, THAT:

1. between 56.8 and 86.0 per cent offer instruction to foremen.

2. between 47.7 and 78.2 per cent offer instruction to junior executives.

3. between 43.3 and 76.7 per cent offer instruction to business professionals.

4. between 32.9 and 66.8 per cent offer instruction to senior executives.

5. between 27.3 and 62.2 per cent offer instruction to factory operatives.

6. between 19.2 and 55.6 per cent offer instruction to the clerical staff.

7. between 1.8 and 39.8 per cent offer instruction to the families of corporation personnel.

III *Integrated Programs*

Having almost burst into existence during the past 10 years, corporation educational programs are still in a dynamic state. Some are just now being established; many are undergoing rapid development; all are subject to abrupt change, as experience and conditions dictate. Differences and similarities appear in bewildering confusion, reflecting various approaches to the problem and the diverse circumstances surrounding each corporation and product. Everywhere there is keen awareness of the acute need for trained personnel, for keeping abreast of the times, and for maintaining a flexible organization. The conviction that the answer is to be found in an educational program is common enough, but there uniformity ends; there is no typical organization, no standard procedure.

This and the following five chapters make a distinction between integrated programs, orientation, and individual courses of instruction. But the distinction is arbitrary; overlapping and subclassification are found. For the purpose of this discussion, however, an integrated program is something more than a course. It is a systematic plan, involving formal or informal instruction, usually both, and designed for some specific end determined by the corporation. The end in view may be managerial and supervisory development, or, in the technical field, a specialized program for graduate engineers, the creation of assistants for engineers, or, perhaps, the training of high-school graduates for certain drafting assignments. Orientation may be considered a special kind of integrated program applicable only to new employees. An individual course of instruction is, as the term indicates, a process of formal instruction developed around a specific body of subject matter and often included in an integrated program, but which may be pursued separately as an end in itself according to individual choice.

Examples from each of these areas are selected for description. The selection is purely fortuitous. Very little of this material is in regularly published form for general distribution. As a result of many personal interviews and voluminous correspondence, however, certain materials, usually in office-duplicated form, have been made available to the authors. It is these that have been used. And it is the belief of the authors, after more than a year of intensive study in preparation for this report, that the collection, even though gathered rather haphazardly, is fairly representative of the courses of study currently being offered by industry in the several areas mentioned.

Managerial and Supervisory

A Personalized Program[1]

This program places prime responsibility upon all personnel of high managerial status for the development of those under their several jurisdictions. It is the task of each such manager to analyze separately every position for which he is responsible, then to list the abilities and characteristics of each incumbent, and finally to compare the results and determine just how each employee can best develop his potential possibilities to the utmost.

The first step, then, calls for the assembly of information concerning the job. What kind of experience is necessary to fill the position adequately—research, supervisory, sales, manufacturing, or something else? What sort of knowledge is required—information concerning managerial techniques, company organization

---

[1] Merck & Company, Inc., Chemical Division, Rahway, N.J., *Management Development Program,* typewritten.

and processes, knowledge of a specialized nature such as accounting, science, engineering, and law, or just a general background of world affairs, political events, economic life, and great literature? What personality traits are desirable—tact in getting along with people, sociability, pride of performance, creative imagination, ability to express oneself effectively? Does the position require proficiency in writing reports, reading blueprints, conducting meetings? Whatever the job calls for in the way of knowledge, personality traits, or skills is recorded.

The second step calls for factual information concerning the present incumbent of the position just analyzed. Besides such routine matters as age, physical appearance, and marital and military status, other pertinent information may be helpful. His community and leisure-time activities may disclose leadership qualities hitherto unnoticed; certainly his work performance, his educational accomplishments, the skills acquired during the course of his career, and his vocational experience are all important. With this task complete, two inventories are at hand, one relating to a specific position, the other to the particular person holding that position.

These two inventories are now compared in the matter of requirements and qualifications. No doubt strong points as well as weak ones are disclosed. This poses the problem of how further to develop proficiency and how to correct shortcomings, all to the end that the individual may attain a full measure of accomplishment.

At this point the manager consults his subordinate, and in many respects this is considered the most crucial step in the program. The purpose is not to create apprehension but to enlarge horizons; not to censure but to help; not merely to improve present performance, but to prepare for future advancement. Having previously studied the two inventories explained above, the manager is in a position to suggest, or perhaps the subordinate may suggest, some systematic self-development program. More specialized or general knowledge may be called for, conceivably unfortunate personality traits may call for correction, or possibly certain skills may need to be developed. Whatever procedure is embarked upon as a result of this conference, the manager retains the functions of adviser and coach. It is he who follows the employee's progress intimately, and it is he who continually supports the development program with assignments which apply the knowledge gained to actual work experience.

And now the company educational department is consulted. If more knowledge of some kind is required, there are courses in mathematics, engineering, science, and similar subjects. If difficulty is experienced in self-expression, public-speaking practice may help. If skills need to be developed, English writing, conference leadership, or rapid-reading instruction is available. Courses of study, conceived and conducted by the company, are flexible, organized as needs develop, and altered as conditions change. Or the employee's interests may better be served through outside educational institutions. If so, the educational department has a complete file of such possibilities and can arrange a short or an extended leave of absence if this seems the thing to do. Nor need the educational assistance necessarily be confined to formal instruction. Books can be supplied from the company library for a reading program if that seems better suited to the occasion, or perhaps the educational director may advise a temporary transfer to some other department where knowledge of company processes, now lacking, can be supplied. Likewise, assignments to special projects or committees, or participation in staff meetings may provide opportunities to augment promising aptitudes or to fill gaps that require attention. Whatever may be decided upon, the educational department supplies the development action part of the program.

In this type of procedure, then, each program is designed for a particular person and proceeds in a systematic manner from analysis through consultation to appropriate action. Nor does it terminate with a single program. Evaluation is repeated at periodic intervals, conferences are held, additional needs determined, and new programs instigated. Education thus becomes a continuing process, a way of life.

Company Correspondence Courses[2]

The interesting feature of this program is that it uses company-organized and -conducted correspondence courses. A total of 39 courses is offered, 26 of which are conducted in this manner. The others are in the nature of seminars. Those eligible may register for the correspondence courses simply by filling out an application card and forwarding it to the company librarian, who then sends the study material directly to the applicant. He prepares and submits answer sheets as time permits. Each is examined, graded, and returned to him in due time. Seminar registrations are handled in a similar manner, except that permission for absences must be obtained from the proper authority. The seminar meetings are scheduled by the education department from time to time during the year. New courses are constantly being added to the curriculum and old ones revised, for no one, it is pointed out, ever arrives at the point where development is complete, especially in a period of rapid change such as the present.

The courses are divided into three main groups—basic, intermediate, and advanced. Each course is assigned a certain number of units, a measure similar in purpose to the point system often used in college curriculums. There are 20 basic courses consisting of 3 seminars and 17 correspondence courses; 10 intermediate courses made up of 3 seminars and 7 correspondence; 9 advanced courses with 7 seminars and 2 correspondence. Employee students, particularly those newly assigned to a supervisory level, are advised to take the basic courses first. Upon successful completion of 50 basic units, together with an additional 83 units selected from the intermediate and advanced groups, a certificate of merit is awarded. Upon the successful completion of 40 additional units, 173 in all, a certificate of merit in advanced supervision is awarded.

As will be seen from the accompanying table, about half the total number of courses offered are assigned to the basic level and

---

[2] General Shoe Corporation, Nashville, Tenn., *Catalogue of Courses and Conferences Offered by the Training Dept. to Help the Supervisor Become a Better Supervisor,* October, 1956.

about a quarter each to the intermediate and advanced levels. The number of seminar courses is the same on the basic and intermediate levels but increases with the advanced level. The number of correspondence courses decreases as the higher levels are reached.

LEVEL DIVISIONS	SEMINAR	CORRESPONDENCE	TOTAL
Basic	3	17	20
Intermediate	3	7	10
Advanced	7	2	9
Total	13	26	39

As might be expected, orientation and material having to do specifically with the company and its products are heavily emphasized on the basic level, the proportion being 3 to 1 in number of courses. On the intermediate level, the proportionate rate shifts to the subjects of a more general nature by 1 to 1½, and on the advanced level, the proportion is 1 to 3½.

LEVEL DIVISIONS	COMPANY	GENERAL	TOTAL
Basic	15	5	20
Intermediate	4	6	10
Advanced	2	7	9
Total	21	18	39

Besides the customary orientation course, company subjects include those of a technical nature dealing with manufacture of the company's product as well as such matters as handling grievances, purchasing, credit, and labor relations. The more general educational subjects include human relations, communication, general supervisory techniques, effective writing, rapid reading, and general business organization.

A graded program is thus offered, but with sufficient latitude in choice of subjects to satisfy individual interests. Through three reasonably defined steps, emphasis is placed progressively upon subjects of a more general nature so essential to management at the higher levels. And concurrently, the seminar technique

replaces correspondence courses, permitting individual personalities to become known. Initiative is left largely to the employees.

Formal Procedure[3]

This program is more rigid in its organization and more
formal in its procedure than either of the two cases considered
thus far. It offers a twofold program—one for managerial training, the other for supervisory development. The first covers a
period of 18 months and is open to a limited number of highly
selected college graduates, preferably with liberal-arts training.
The second is offered to several hundred supervisors and is conducted from September to June each year. Both are conducted on
company time, with no expenses to the participants other than
textbooks, and these are supplied at cost.

Each January and June about 12 recruits are selected for the
managerial training course. At all times 36 men are training, and
24 are graduated each year. After a brief period of orientation,
they are given machine-shop practice. This is conducted in a
vestibule school where the men can learn various processes involved in the manufacture of the product by actually performing
them, but without interruption to the regular flow of production,
and with full-time instructors always at hand to explain and to
help. The vestibule school is under continuous operation. A new
entering class begins as soon as the old one passes on to the second
stage of the training.

The second stage consists of classroom work. A definite schedule of hours is assigned, with intervening periods of study, together occupying an 8-hour day. The teaching staff is composed
of personnel from the training division as well as from various
departments of the plant, depending upon the subject presented.
Standard college textbooks are used, as well as specially prepared
material. Some of the subjects have to do particularly with company work as, for example, manufacturing processes, labor contract, inspection procedures, cost accounting, budget control, company organization, and interdepartmental instructions. Some of

[3] Information furnished through the courtesy of the Curtiss-Wright Corporation, Wright Aeronautical Division, Wood-Ridge, N.J.

the more general subjects considered are metallurgy, statistics, manufacturing engineering, personnel administration, basic electricity, engineering economy, and slide-rule computations.

The final stage in this managerial training course consists of project assignments alternated with classroom work. An assignment is some special research or investigation which needs to be done, but for which no one is immediately available. It is on-the-job training but not in an established post. The projects occupy from 2 to 17 weeks, each man being assigned 3 or 4 in different operating divisions of the company. Collectively, a given class may have as many as 44 project assignments. The company reports many valuable contributions resulting from this procedure. It is said to give the trainee an opportunity to become acquainted with various operations of the company similar to the on-the-job rotation practiced in other cases, and to give the executives in charge of the various divisions an opportunity to become acquainted with and to evaluate the work of the trainees.

Beginning with the initial interview, each trainee is evaluated at periodic intervals throughout the course of training. Personality traits such as initiative, tact, aggressiveness, and so forth, are considered. This is done by the training managers as well as by the men themselves, each being required to rate himself and all other members of the class, thus preparing them in an important managerial function—that of evaluating others. The training director considers the combined results in personal interviews with the trainees and can often make suggestions for correcting shortcomings and improving general performance.

Upon completion of the course, the men are assigned to definite posts, and from then on their progress is reviewed in surveys made from time to time. If the training programs warrant the investment necessary per man, then the graduates should advance farther and faster than the normal rate of progression, and the records show that they do.

The supervisory development program is conducted entirely by college professors and is conducted on a formal basis. A contract with a nearby university provides that several members of the college staff spend a large part of their time at the company plant.

The participants, several hundred in number, are selected by their department managers for possessing the requisite ability, personality, and ambition for advancement. The program is given in several sections from September to June, once a week, on company time. The courses offered follow closely those customarily required of candidates for a baccalaureate degree in business, for example, business writing, industrial psychology, conference methods, cost control and accounting, business organization, statistics, budget control, and production planning. Standard college textbooks are used and are sold to the participants at cost. Otherwise, all expense is borne by the company. Regular examinations are administered, and grades are assigned.

This dual program is more intensive than any thus far considered. Directed as it is to a highly selected group and to experienced employees, it concentrates on a rigid course of instruction not unlike that of a technical college curriculum as far as procedure is concerned.

Personal and Formal

This case incorporates some features of all three programs described above. Candidates are rigidly selected, then serve a sort of apprenticeship under various company personnel who provide personal guidance. Formal education is given through correspondence courses, in this instance administered by the International Correspondence School, but no selection is permitted. There are also formal classroom courses, and, in addition, considerable experience is provided in group meetings, conferences, and consultations.

The program provides that the manufacturing supervisors and the labor-relations department constantly survey the working force for administrative talent. Upon suggestion, or his own initiative, a candidate for the managerial development program submits a formal application supported by recommendations from his immediate superiors. His work record, scholastic accomplishments, outside interests, and general background are investigated, and various psychological tests are administered as aids in determining mental alertness, personality traits, vocational interests, aptitudes, and other pertinent data. The employee is finally interviewed by various supervisors and executives, and, if accepted as a candidate, he is so notified in writing. The number of candidates thus selected is determined by a periodic estimate of the vacancies in prospect from retirement, promotion, and expansion. This estimate is then broken down into annual quotas which indicate the number and nature of the vacancies to be filled.

The program consists of two parts; all candidates successfully completing the first part are either immediately assigned responsible manufacturing posts or continue on to the second part of the program. Only those who have demonstrated outstanding ability during the first part of the training are selected to continue on to the second.

Part 1 of the program covers a period of 6 months and consists of (1) general studies in the form of assigned readings and ICS courses, (2) specific instruction in company operations as managerial apprentices, (3) classroom discussions in which information concerning company techniques is alternated with instruction in subjects of a general nature, and (4) attendance at regional managerial conferences. General studies include such material as factory organization and administration, industrial engineering, business psychology, industrial relations, supervision techniques, office management, public speaking, and human relations. Instruction in company operations includes a comprehensive schedule of actual work experiences in all phases of the manufacture of the company product, in the course of which the candidate is assigned a series of supervisory responsibilities of increasing importance. Besides classroom instruction having to do particularly with the company product, 15 or 16 discussions are devoted to leadership training, including a consideration of productivity, communication, safety, grievances, discipline, absenteeism, teaching, and teamwork. During the period of training, the candidates are required to attend regular meetings conducted by the American Management Association and the National Industrial Conference Board.

Part 2 of the managerial development program is a 13-week program for those who are selected to continue their training.

During this period the candidate is assigned actual work functions in some 13 different divisions of the corporation, each for a period of 1 week. These include general and cost accounting, purchasing, industrial engineering, labor relations, legal matters, testing, research and development, new products, traffic, and sales.

Evaluation is continuous throughout the program. Each candidate is required to submit a weekly activities report to various executives concerned with the program. This report includes subjects taken up during the week, hours spent in study, conferences and consultations, and participation in any outside activities. Each supervisor having a candidate under his jurisdiction submits a rating sheet weekly, covering evaluation of the quality and quantity of work accomplished, initiative and resourcefulness demonstrated, ability to work with others, comprehension of task assigned, and general attitudes demonstrated. The sheet also requires percentage ratings covering personality traits such as punctuality, appropriate behavior, and understanding of company policies. The local plant manager holds weekly conferences with each trainee under his authority, and each trainee is required to appear before a monthly foremen's meeting and present some topic which he has prepared on his own initiative.

Throughout the program the employee-relations department and the vice-president in charge of training review monthly the record of each trainee. Upon completion of the training, the graduate is awarded a certificate of completion and is assigned a permanent position.

Understudy Training[4]

The term "understudy" indicates the nature of the procedure. Each individual of supervisory status assumes responsibility for coaching a subordinate next in authority to assume the supervisory post. The subordinate is therefore in a position at any time to substitute in the absence of his superior or to replace him should the superior move up in the hierarchical ladder. Definite motivation is thus provided the understudy, while the superior's chances

[4] Glenn L. Martin Company, Baltimore, Md., *Understudy Training,* a brochure.

for promotion are enhanced because of the assurance of continuous succession. Then, too, the very process of coaching may
highlight aspects of the job that would otherwise be overlooked,
absences cause no embarrassment, and time is released for over-all
planning and self-development. The understudy need not at once
be informed of his selection. Tests and comparisons are advised,
and constant coaching of all subordinates is encouraged. But
sooner or later an understudy is chosen and groomed to assume
the higher post.

The coaching involves various techniques. Delegation of authority is essential, carefully controlled, of course, because responsibility cannot be shifted. Decision making, problem solving,
experience in dealing with others, and representing his superior
in various meetings become a regular part of the subordinate's
daily work schedule, thus giving him the opportunity of proving
himself capable of promotion.

In addition, the subordinate may be recommended for a training program open to selected personnel from various departments
and designed to prepare them for first-level supervisory positions
as opportunities occur. Training groups of 15 or 20 individuals
are formed to receive formal instruction for 2 sessions of 2 hours
each a week. The performance of each trainee is evaluated, and
his superior is kept informed of the progress made. Supervisors
are also advised of the subjects considered in the classroom from
session to session, in order that they may review the topics with
the trainees and synchronize the classroom work as closely as
possible with on-the-job experience.

Subjects considered in the classroom include company organization, job-planning instruction and assignments, accident prevention, absentee control, labor relations, communication, and human
relations. These subjects are taught by company supervisors from
the various departments having to do with the particular subject
in question.

It will be seen that this plan is similar to the first case considered, except for the understudy concept. The preliminary
evaluations are not so closely defined, however, while the subse-

quent procedure is more rigid, particularly the presupervisory training for which the subordinate may be recommended.

Technical Programs

Keeping Up to Date

Once inducted into the technical intricacies of a given industry, there is the problem of keeping abreast of the new inventions, improved methods, and pioneer developments constantly emerging from research and experience. Meetings of professional societies, technical publications, and informal contacts all contribute, but many companies provide a more systematic and formal procedure. To this end, one company employs engineering professors from nearby universities, and the company engineers attend their courses during the day on company time. The subject matter varies according to need and current developments, as does the time allotment. Classes may be held several hours a day or two or three times a week.

Another company[5] provides a twofold program—company-time and after-hours seminars. The first are held intermittently and are restricted to invited personnel. Topics having to do with the latest developments involving the company's product are discussed, sometimes by company engineers and scientists, sometimes by visiting specialists from industry or the universities. After-hours seminars are held weekly and are open to all engineering personnel. Some current development in the industry is presented by a guest speaker, followed by an hour of questions and discussion.

Graduate Engineering Program[6]

As these lines are being written, a new graduate engineering program is being announced. Quarters in New York consist of classrooms, conference rooms, laboratories, and a restaurant. Comparable facilities are being established in Chicago and Winston-Salem, North Carolina. The project is the equivalent in cost and

[5] Information furnished through the courtesy of the International Business Machines Corporation, New York.

[6] The Western Electric Company, Inc., adapted from an article in the *New York Times,* June 15, 1957.

administration, it is said, of a new engineering school of 1,000 full-time students. The original outlay is reported to have cost $1,000,000, and the annual operating expenses are estimated at $2,000,000.

Instruction is offered on three levels: introductory, covering basic communication systems, engineering functions, and product design offered to young engineers who have been with the company for 6 months to 1 year; general development courses; and advanced technical subjects dealing with current developments in communication engineering. The teaching staff is drawn partly from corporation personnel and partly from leading universities, the latter numbering about 70 persons. Co-operating universities are: Cornell, Duke, North Carolina State, Illinois Institute of Technology, Northwestern, and New York Universities.

Developing Assistant Engineers[7]

To help fill the gap between the demand for graduate engineers and the relatively limited supply, this company offers a 12-week course of 40 hours a week to laboratory technicians who hold a 2-year technical diploma or the equivalent in military or industrial experience. This training is designed to develop assistants who may assume some of the duties normally performed by technical graduates. The program is allotted 470 hours, 280 to classroom lectures, demonstrations, and discussions, and 190 to laboratory work. Enrollment is limited to 20 students to a class. Two full-time instructors are assigned to the course, one for classroom instruction, the other to the laboratory. Various company personnel are drawn upon for special presentations. Standard textbooks as well as specially prepared materials are used.

Making Draftsmen[8]

Descending another rung in the hierarchical ladder of technical training is a program designed to train high-school graduates in

[7] Information furnished through the courtesy of the International Business Machines Corporation, New York.

[8] Information furnished through the courtesy of the Timken Roller Bearing Company, Canton, Ohio.

drafting. The procedure is not unlike that of shop apprenticeship. By continuing study, particularly in the area of college mathematics, the student draftsman may become a "master," or fullfledged draftsman, in 6 years. The trainee is first given classroom instruction in mathematics and drafting. He is then assigned to an engineering department where a rotation of duties is arranged, the student moving from group to group as each task is completed satisfactorily. In each group the supervisor acts as instructor, teaching the work of that particular group. Compensation is that of a high-school graduate at the start, and is increased annually. Upon completion of the program, the trainee is assigned to the engineering department for permanent employment.

A subsidiary program of similar nature is open to women. A high-school diploma is prerequisite. The girls join the company as tracers, and take company courses extending over a period of $1\frac{1}{2}$ years. Eventually, they are classified as third-grade draftsmen and are assigned to the engineering department.

IV *Orientation*

Not so long ago when a new employee was hired he was put directly to work in his assigned task. From that time on, he shifted for himself, learning the job by trial and error, finding his way around by observing others, making chance acquaintances as best he could, and being subject to all the disquieting rumors that are frequently an integral part of shop and office gossip. Labor turnover among new employees, however, was found to be high, sometimes nearly five times as high for those with less than 1 month's standing as for those who remained 1 to 3 months.[1] Each turnover, it is said, costs from $50 to $500. It takes only 100 replacements, then, at a cost of, say, $250 each, to equal a 10 per cent profit on sales amounting to $250,000.[2] No wonder some better method had to be found!

Today there are few establishments of any size without an orientation program of some kind. For the factory worker it may consist of an explanation of company rules and policies, followed by introductions, instructions, and helpful information given by the supervisor. For highly trained technical positions, it may continue as long as 2 years, during which time the new employee is rotated from one position to another, thus becoming acquainted with the activities of the corporation as a whole before being assigned a permanent place in it. In such cases, orientation supple-

[1] Norman R. F. Maier, *Principles of Human Relations,* John Wiley & Sons, Inc., New York, 1952, p. 390.

[2] *Personnel,* American Management Association, New York, March, 1953, p. 408.

ments an integrated educational training program such as those described in the last chapter. For others, a week or so may be given over to getting acquainted before regular positions are assigned or formal training begins.

Orientation for New Factory Workers[3]

In one plant, new factory workers first report to the employment office where the receptionist collects their documents, such as admission passes, birth certificates, social security cards, and so on. These are sent to the identification office where permanent badges are prepared. In the meantime, the workers assemble in a classroom. Here the men receive an official welcome. Company regulations are explained, safety and security measures are described, and the suggestion system, designed by the company to facilitate upward communication, is explained. During this class session the various departments to which the new workers have been assigned are notified, and messengers are dispatched to show the new workers their respective work areas. From that point on, the foremen or supervisors take over the details of introduction, instructions, and follow-up.

A Week of Orientation[4]

Another company brings together all of its newly acquired college graduates, both engineers and others, in some centrally located plant for a week of intensive orientation. During this period, observations and lectures cover a cross section of all the important operations, policies, and plans of the company.

At the outset there are introductory talks by various company officials. The history of the corporation is reviewed, its various products and markets are explained, its organizational structure is analyzed, and its future plans and objectives are outlined. The men learn about the company's various plants—their locations, size, and what each contributes to the organization as a whole.

[3] Information furnished through the courtesy of Curtiss-Wright Corporation, Wright Aeronautical Division, Wood-Ridge, N.J.
[4] Armstrong Cork Company, Lancaster, Pa., *Introductory Week*, typewritten.

The different manufacturing divisions are explained, and their finished products are examined. The markets for each are pointed out, consideration being given to the number and location of company sales offices and such distributor relationships as exist.

At another time a study is made of the corporation's accounting, financial, secretarial, and legal activities. The controller's office, it is discovered, is concerned with much more than merely past business operations. It evaluates future plans and analyzes the results of plans already in process, noting deviations not contemplated and indicating corrective measures which are thought possible. Here also, estimates of future sales are compiled, and calculations of statistical relationships such as profit to sales, turnover of sales to average assets, and the returns from capital invested are made. Likewise, the office of the treasurer is seen to involve more than the receipt and disbursement of funds. Here, economic and commercial research such as forecasting business conditions and estimating future markets is carried on. The office of secretary, it is learned, is not only the custodian of corporate records but cares for federal, state, and local tax problems, insurance operations, and real-estate purchases and sales. Through its legal department the secretary's office is also charged with the responsibility of matters concerning patents, trade-marks, and copyrights, as well as general legal matters such as passing upon company contracts, investigating labor legislation, and keeping abreast of antitrust laws.

Consideration of the functions of the engineering department follows. This office, it seems, is responsible for the supervision and maintenance of fixed capital investments such as buildings, machinery, and other equipment. Such problems as those having to do with refuse disposal, dust elimination, and scrap disposition also come within the scope of its work. Evolving new products is a particularly important activity, and the procedures involved are explained.

The first thing that the men learn when they hear about the company's employee relations is that nowhere are the policies and practices pursued by the company more important than in this area. Technical proficiency, ideal working conditions, even liberal compensation can all be offset by neglect or poor performance in this division. Here, problems involving human relations are considered, and the men are shown how complex they become with rapid company expansion. For this reason, increasing emphasis is being put upon them. Procedures conducive to good employee relations such as orientation, education, upgrading, and effective upward communication are explained. How effective such measures are is revealed by research projects constantly being carried on to check the procedures and practices being pursued.

Finally, the men are informed regarding the sales, advertising, and public-relations activities of the company. These include the export division, where affiliations in various parts of the world are explained.

Technical Orientation[5]

A large oil company provides an orientation program, covering a period of approximately 4 months, for its newly acquired engineers and chemists. The timing differs somewhat for the two groups, but the sequence of observations and studies is the same.

At the outset, 1 month is spent in one of the refineries, the time being apportioned among the major processing units where operational, engineering, and maintenance problems are reviewed. Special equipment and other installations in use are studied, and the sequence in which the various refining operations take place and the daily changes in procedures are observed and explained. The laboratory is visited daily, where checks of flow rates are compared with experimental data.

This is followed by a few days of lectures and discussions covering the company's history, organization, financial position, and policies. At this time, special emphasis is placed upon fire protection, safety measures, and accident prevention.

The engineers spend 2 weeks or more, and the chemists a few days, in the engineering department. Here new construction and current maintenance are studied, with particular reference to planning, timing and estimating, selection and ordering of ma-

[5] Tidewater Oil Company, Avon Refinery, *Technical Training Program,* typewritten.

terials, the preparation of contracts, and the relations of the departments with outside contractors. Here the newly employed engineers are assigned minor engineering projects, thus gaining actual on-the-job experience under the close supervision of an engineer group leader.

Following their work in the engineering department, a few days are spent in the storehouse, in the fields with surveyors, and in the drafting room. In the storehouse the men see how requisitions are handled, how inventories are kept at even levels, and how the routine for ordering special materials, not usually stocked, is handled. In the field a study is made involving the location of equipment, determination of necessary piping, and other information needed when opening up a new area of operations. In the drafting room the routine for handling drawings is explained, and the men become familiar with the co-operative relationships between the engineers and the draftsmen.

The inspection department, the maintenance and construction department, the control laboratories, and procedures involving research and development now occupy the attention of the men for several weeks. One week is spent with a plant inspector checking refinery equipment; several more weeks are given to studying plans and operations having to do with current maintenance and new construction. The work in the control laboratories, of more interest to the chemists than the engineers, is concerned with the checking of manufactured products against agreed-upon specifications. Both engineers and chemists spend several weeks in the various divisions concerned with research and development, studying new developments in Diesel fuel and automotive and aviation gasoline, and how new processes are devised and the ones in current use improved.

Observations in the utility, gauging and shipping, and packaging and blending departments take up somewhat over 2 weeks. In the first of these, the operational and engineering problems having to do with boilerhouse, waste, and water-treating systems are studied. In the second, the duties and responsibilities of the oil dispatcher, the chief gauger, and the plant gaugers are observed, and in the third, such operations as grease making and ethyl blending, as well as methods employed in loading tank cars, trucks, and trailers, are investigated.

The chemists now spend a few weeks in the technology department where investigations of various products are constantly in process. Here they assist in the blending of various kinds of fuels. Here also they see how economic conditions in the petroleum industry are studied and forecasts of the future demand and supply of various products are prepared—essential data for management in planning for the future.

Toward the end of the orientation period, the men are made familiar with office procedures such as the scheduling of foreign and domestic crude-oil receipts, the preparation of legal papers, and accounting practices.

Engineer Orientation[6]

Engineers entering the employ of this company are assigned to a general engineering training program on an individual basis. Particular courses are selected for each trainee in the light of his previous education and experience as well as his position in prospect.

The program usually starts the latter part of July, following graduation. It consists of four parts. Part 1 considers company policies and practices and engineering organization and functions having to do with the company's commercial and military products. Part 2 consists of a field assignment. This may be to a branch office or to a field operation, depending upon the particular schedule determined for the trainee. Part 3 involves, first, technical courses in the mechanical field, such as machine design, mechanical instrumentation, manufacturing and assembly practices, and other such topics; and second, courses in the electrical field including principles of digital and analog computers, organization of data-processing machines, a military product system, consideration of computer circuit design, circuit logic, electric packaging practices, and related subjects. Part 4 is applied to personal

[6] Information furnished through the courtesy of the International Business Machines Corporation, New York.

development. Technical report writing, conference leadership, and creative engineering are some of the topics included.

The schedule calls for full-time training for from 2 to 8 weeks. The field assignment is completed sometime between the end of Part 1 and the termination of the program. The balance of the program is arranged on a part-time basis varying from 2 to 4 hours a day. A typical program covers a period of 34 weeks.

The teaching is conducted by staff instructors, senior engineers, plant managers, and specialists on specific subjects. Teaching methods include class demonstrations, discussions, recitations, practice problems, class-conducted seminars, and plant visits. Each trainee is rated on fundamental abilities, personal characteristics, and performance. These are determined by examinations, personal conferences, oral questioning, practice problem assignments, and observations of the trainee's participation in class activities, his disposition to co-operate, and his willingness to accept responsibility. Upon completion of the program, he is awarded a certificate at a formal graduation ceremony.

Orientation courses are many and varied, but all have the common objective of giving new employees an over-all view of the corporation and its activities. When assigned a definite post, then, each man sees himself not as an isolated individual performing tasks more or less meaningless when viewed apart from the whole but as a vital part of a closely integrated organization to which his own efforts make a significant contribution.

v A Course in Managerial and Supervisory Development

Management, it is said, is being judged increasingly by its ability to give work satisfaction.[1] This means more than a mere livelihood, even at high wages; it implies psychic income, a sense of participation, of being needed, of playing a significant role in some worthwhile undertaking, and the realization that there exists an opportunity for growth and development to the utmost extent of one's capacities. A study made 7 years ago (1950), in which interviews were held with more than 1,000 persons representing a cross section of the American public, reported that almost 50 per cent expressed the opinion that big business paid higher wages than small business; in the matter of attitude toward employees, however, less than 7 per cent felt that big-business management surpassed that of small business.[2] Such opinions reflect the policies pursued in an era when management's activities, particularly in big business, were concentrated on production, and workers were looked upon as mere instruments to that end; when the daily life in a factory took on the aspects of a ceaseless battle against what was considered a natural disinclination to put in a fair day's work; when personal problems, maladjustments, frustrations, and hostile attitudes, even if known to exist, were regarded as quite beyond the province of an industrial establishment.

[1] Eugene Staley (Ed.), *Creating an Industrial Civilization, a Report on the Corning Conference,* Harper & Brothers, New York, 1952, p. 37.

[2] Burton H. Fisher and Stephen H. Withey, *Big Business as the People See It,* The Survey Research Center, University of Michigan, Ann Arbor, Mich., 1951, p. 98.

Since that time a veritable revolution in regard to such matters has taken place. Today, progressive corporations are employee-centered, workers are respected as individuals, and the factory, although still a hierarchical institution, is looked upon as a social system, however vast and complex, offering individuals work satisfaction and personal fulfillment as participants in creative activity.[3] Nowhere are these revised policies better shown than in what is being taught in courses in managerial and supervisory development conducted by industry.

Imagine a comfortable and well-equipped classroom, perhaps in the main plant, perhaps in a building apart. There are modern blackboards, stands for visual materials, projection equipment, and sound recording machines. The class (one in actual existence while this is being written) is composed of 25 supervisors of various levels. Meetings are held on company time for $1\frac{1}{2}$ hours every week for 16 weeks, comparable to a 1-semester college course. The course is divided into two sections: the first, covering 13 weeks, considers managerial and supervisory skills applicable to almost any business; the second, covering 3 weeks, deals with information concerning a particular company. The 13 sessions of the first section are summarized in this chapter. Thus the subject matter considered in this particular course, as well as the teaching methods used in this and similar courses, can be judged.

A Course for Supervisors[4]

First Session

After a few introductory remarks concerning the growth and increasing complexity of industry, the instructor poses the question, "Why is supervision more difficult today?"

Many reasons are suggested: labor unions, increased knowledge necessary, more demands from the men, high-speed scheduling, and so on. The more important points are listed on the blackboard. The discussion leads to the conclusion that the demands of the job today can be met only through specialized training.

[3] Eugene Staley, *op. cit.,* p. 175.
[4] Johnson & Johnson, New Brunswick, N.J., *Fundamentals of Management,* Aug. 1, 1955, typewritten.

The functions and responsibilities of a supervisor are now compared with the results of a survey analyzing the weak and strong points of supervision in current operation in the plant. Office-duplicated sheets explaining different types of supervisors are distributed, and the discussion ends on a note of self-analysis: "What kind of a supervisor are you?"

Second Session

A 35-minute motion picture introduces the second session. It illustrates the four basic drives common to all human beings acting in groups: (1) belonging, (2) recognition, (3) new experience, and (4) security.

Graphic illustrations are now used to center attention upon these basic drives, one at a time, while the group is asked to apply them to actual job situations. *Belonging,* it is suggested, may be fostered by orientation programs, group meetings, athletic events, parties, and group incentives; *recognition* by a supervisor's interest displayed in an individual as such, commendation when due, merit ratings, and promotion when earned; *new experience* by job rotation, enlarged responsibilities, and, when warranted, work on committees and education; *security* by low labor turnover, pensions, insurance benefits, and the dissemination of complete information regarding anticipated plans involving changes necessary to meet new opportunities. The leader points out that these basic drives, when blocked, can create maladjustments and engender general discontent with both the job and the company, resulting in decreased productivity. The group concludes that failure to create a sense of belonging, for example, might well cause loneliness; that a prolonged period on a monotonous job would certainly result in boredom; that a lack of recognition for deserved accomplishments could easily arouse a feeling of neglect; and that fear and worry are certainly the counterparts of insecurity. It is agreed that such matters all fall within the general category of morale. Morale, then, is correlated intimately and positively with productivity. The results of surveys aimed to discover the existing morale in the plant are now presented and evaluated by the group.

At the end of the session, appropriate readings are suggested, extracts from which are distributed. There are distributed also lists of important points brought out in the course of the discussion and definite suggestions for applying the knowledge gained to actual work conditions.

Third Session

Organization begins when one person has more to do than he alone can handle, but problems arise when he gets others to help him. These can be resolved or avoided by following principles or generalizations crystallized from long experience. This session considers some of these principles.

The leader distributes a paper describing the habits of a hypothetical manager whom the group is asked to rate as excellent, average, or poor. The papers are then collected, but will be returned at the end of the period for revision. Perhaps, after a discussion of the principles, some may wish to change their minds, and many do. Introducing Principle Number One, the leader poses the question, "How many employees can a supervisor handle directly?" The group decides that this depends upon circumstances such as whether the work is repetitive or not, the experience of the workers, the ability of the supervisors in handling subordinates, and the level of supervision. But always there is a limit. Then what? This raises the question of delegation or transfer of responsibility, and the discussion leads to Principle Number Two: Authority must be commensurate with responsibility. Delegation, it is pointed out, is often resisted, and reasons for this, such as urge for personal power, reluctance to admit limitations, and desire to avoid responsibility for the work of others, are cited. Continued discussion, prompted and guided by comments and occasional questions by the leader, highlights six other principles of organization: (1) A superior is responsible for the acts of a subordinate. (2) A subordinate receives instruction from only one person higher in authority. (3) Supervisors act jointly only with the consent of their superior. (4) Duties, authority, and responsibilities must be closely defined. (5) Assignments must be similar at a given level, and not too numerous.

(6) Managerial effectiveness is increased when confined to matters other than those involved in ordinary routine.

Fourth Session

Communication, in an industrial organization, consists of the dissemination of information, instructions, explanations, and company rules downward from management to the employees, and the voicing of ideas, opinions, or just feelings about the job and the company upward from those same employees to management. This sounds simple enough, but it becomes a complicated process where thousands of widely scattered employees are involved. With some such remarks, the leader introduces the subject of this fourth session of the course in the fundamentals of management. And he adds, with emphasis, that free communication both downward and upward is essential to modern management. Downward communication establishes confidence by releasing company news and explaining plans and policies in the making before rumor becomes rife and perhaps disquieting. It engenders loyalty by describing company research, organization, forthcoming advertising campaigns, and increased sales, and it gives management an opportunity to keep the organization receptive to the change so essential in a period of dynamic development. Upward communication permits employees to make suggestions for increased efficiency, to voice their understanding of new instructions, and to express their opinions regarding company policies.

The functions and importance of communication in industry thus having been explained, the leader now asks the group to name some impediments to both downward and upward communication. Among the first, the problem of interpretation is advanced, that is, the difficulty of overcoming emotional barriers to the end that the message received conveys to the recipient the same meaning intended by the sender. Someone suggests that if free upward communication exists, management can gauge the extent to which its messages are comprehended and accepted. This, the leader remarks, is an excellent point. All agree, however, that upward communication is difficult. Reluctance to voice criticism, awkward self-expression, lack of encouragement, perhaps habits of inattention or inaction on the part of management—all are impediments to free upward communication.

At this point a list of general rules designed to facilitate communication is distributed, and the barriers previously listed are reviewed in the light of these rules. Finally, as the session ends, summaries of recent surveys made at the plant for the purpose of discovering the effectiveness of the company's present communication techniques are distributed.

Fifth Session

At the outset of the fifth meeting of the class, papers are distributed showing figures on labor turnover in various corporations. Invariably, according to these figures, turnover is high among low-seniority employees and particularly high among those serving less than 1 year. All agree that the manner in which a new employee is received and introduced to his job determines in large measure whether or not he will remain; first impressions are lasting impressions.

The leader remarks that a new employee must feel needed and wanted and must be given a sense of being accepted by his work group. "What do you do," he asks, "to induct a new employee?"

The ensuing discussion is summed up in a chart showing a sequence of things that can be done. For example, greet the new employee cordially, find out his interests in a friendly chat, explain the job he is about to undertake, and inform him concerning the rules and regulations that apply to it. Show him where he will work, the location of lockers, cafeteria, and rest rooms; introduce him to his co-workers, particularly the union steward, then place him under the direction of a competent instructor.

The chart is supported by a check list, now distributed, showing a more detailed breakdown of procedures to follow when a new employee joins the company. The leader points out that this original introduction must be followed up by keeping the employee informed of any changes that affect him, and making sure that he is recognized as a co-worker by his associates. An important phase in this process of induction, it is explained, consists of acquainting the new employee with the company's history, organization, and policies, displaying samples of the company's products and explaining the training courses available to the workers.

The session ends with a case study demonstrating about every wrong way to treat a new employee. The group criticizes the procedure thus described, in the light of the previous comments and discussion.

Sixth Session

Whatever educational opportunities are offered by a corporation, it is still the job of management to teach. This, the leader explains, is the subject of the present session.

"What is learning?" he asks.

The responses of the group are summed up in the word "change." Learning changes ideas, habits, and attitudes.

And what is teaching? It is arranging situations designed to bring about a desired change.

Individuals in the class are asked to recall their first day on a new job. One mentions confusion, another fear; another remarks that he made many mistakes; others confess that they felt nervous, stupid, and unenthusiastic.

These situations are common, the leader explains, and can be met by patience, a spirit of helpfulness, showing interest in an employee's difficulties, expressing confidence in his ability to overcome them, demonstrating the skills to be mastered, and offering sympathetic criticism as the employee practices with them.

The laws of learning are now explained, and each is summed up by some easily remembered phrase. Motivation—think of appeals to children and animals; meaningful material—start with the familiar; receptivity—put the worker at ease; activity—have the worker perform; accuracy—teach the right way first; appeals—make use of all five senses; repetition—strange ideas and skills soon become familiar; timing—avoid fatigue; curiosity— tell the employee how he is getting along and reassure him at intervals.

Sheets are now distributed relating these laws of learning to laws of teaching, and, using these laws of teaching as a base, the group now completes the session with a list of the qualities desirable for job instructors.

Seventh Session

The seventh session begins with these words placed on the blackboard: "planning," "commanding," "controlling," "improving." These are the functions of management, it is explained, and the present session has to do with commanding or giving orders. Sheets recounting a short case study are distributed, and time is given to consider it. What was the trouble in this case?

Someone suggests that the order was not clear. This is discussed, and all agree that an order must at least be simple and complete, with the receiver repeating it as a check, because what the supervisor actually says, what he thinks he says, and what the receiver hears may all be different.

How about acceptability? Does the receiver need to agree that the order is justified and practical and to feel, perhaps, that it is a challenge to his abilities? Some say "no," that an order is an order—no back talk.

But what about morale, considered in a previous session? Are security and recognition involved in giving an order, and if so, will not the order be carried out more effectively and efficiently if high morale is maintained? The question is hardly debatable. Then it is suggested that good practice dictates that an employee be told why an order is given, how it can be carried out, and the authority for issuing it, making sure all the while, of course, that the task assigned is consistent with the skill and experience of the recipient.

The matter of tact in giving an order is now considered in more detail. Another paper, naming certain common characteristics noted in workers and how to cope with them, is distributed. Some can stand being hurried and like it; others are more deliberate and need time to comprehend; some are indecisive and need help in the form of definite suggestions on how to proceed. Sometimes it is better to let the receiver believe that he is making all the decisions himself. Sometimes irrelevant discussions need to be sidetracked, or cynicism and suspicion just ignored.

The session closes with the distribution of a third paper suggesting when verbal orders are better and when orders should be written.

Eighth Session

Role playing is now introduced as a teaching device. This requires a few words of explanation by the leader concerning its use and effectiveness. The particular skit presented on this occasion shows a supervisor rudely reprimanding a worker, within the hearing of others, for being late to work. After the first outburst, the supervisor learns that a genuine emergency caused the tardiness. Now he shifts the reprimand to something else, errors in the worker's reports, and terminates the interview in a high-handed manner.

The faults of such a procedure are listed: The reprimand was given in public; the supervisor did not listen and hence did not know the facts; then he changed the reprimand to something wholly irrelevant to the first point at issue, all the while displaying ill will and anger.

Constructive suggestions for reprimanding are now listed on the blackboard under three headings: "before," "during," and "after." Subheadings include "know the facts," "have in mind a corrective procedure," "proceed in a friendly manner," "sandwich the reprimand between commendations," "follow up afterward with casual contacts." A paper enumerating certain principles of reprimanding, such as privacy, calmness, consistency, regard for personal traits, attention directed to the error rather than to the person committing it, prompt discipline appropriate to the offense, and emphasis placed upon corrective measures, is now distributed. Finally, the attention of the group is directed to case studies, each presenting a different kind of situation calling for a reprimand, and each suggesting a different solution. The principles already suggested are applied in seeking solutions.

Ninth Session

Wherever men work together, friendships will be formed and, at the same time, misunderstandings will occur; antagonisms may arise, and even enmities may develop, affecting morale and taking toll of productivity. Someone must hear complaints even if they are unjustified; must ferret them out even when they remain unexpressed. This is an important function of management, as explained by the leader in this ninth meeting of the class. As in the previous lesson, it starts with a skit showing a supervisor's handling of a complaint, and the group is asked to criticize the methods used. A plan is then proposed for the proper handling of complaints. To facilitate the discussion, a paper is distributed which outlines the various steps to be followed: (1) Listen—don't argue. This is so important that a supplementary sheet elaborating upon this point is distributed. (2) Consider the facts and be willing to admit mistakes. (3) Make a decision in accordance with established practices but avoid any hasty judgment. (4) Explain the decision. (5) Follow it up in order to check the results.

The session ends with a consideration of problems in the form of case studies.

Tenth Session

Employee counseling involves more than the mere hearing of complaints and administering of reprimands considered in the last two sessions. Personalities are in a constant state of flux and change; some individuals grow in emotional maturity; others are thwarted by maladjustments which impede their work and progress. High morale and productivity can be maintained only by encouraging those who show promise and by helping others who falter. An even flow of normal development among the personnel thus calls for continuous counseling. The leader goes on to explain that the techniques of good counseling can be acquired through learning and practice. The counselor must be versed, for example, in the fundamentals of human behavior. He must know that people are motivated through wants, and that they are frustrated in the process of obtaining these wants because of various circumstances, ofttimes obstructions placed in the way by other people. Maybe their own defects hold them back; sometimes conflicting motives cancel out all possibilities of progress. Adjustment takes place when such conditions are accepted as the normal conditions of life. Maladjustments can and do develop, however, causing mental disorder—neurotic if mild, psychoneurotic if more severe, psychotic if extremely severe. Mental disorders may take the form of anxiety and fear, an effort to escape from reality, cycles of exaltation and depression, or indulgence in fantasies.

The group is asked to cite examples of maladjustment. Someone is oversensitive perhaps, or habitually late to work, accident prone, or confused when required to work under pressure. A supervisor may be a bully or a faultfinder, or he may be over-meticulous concerning trivial details. An effort is made to trace these examples back to their underlying causes. Knowledge of human behavior is thus seen to be one essential qualification of a good counselor, for causes rather than symptoms must be corrected. In addition, it is pointed out, he must be a well-adjusted individual himself, must be objective and sensitive to social situations, and must have respect for individual personalities no matter what form they may take.

Specific problems are now placed before the group in the form of film strips, and papers giving helpful hints as to how people react to common situations are distributed.

Eleventh Session

Employees must be periodically rated. Such ratings are necessary to show whether or not improvement is taking place, what training is desirable, when a promotion, transfer, or advance is warranted, and to provide a check on the selection of future employees. Some formal system is necessary in order to assure the greatest possible objectivity and accuracy in assigning ratings. After some such introductory remarks, the leader proceeds to explain the different kinds of rating systems.

There is a check-list method, calling for an estimate in figures from 0 to 5 on each of a number of specific characteristics such as quality and quantity of work, thoroughness, neatness, judg-

ment, co-operation, initiative, ability to understand, and so on.
The sum of the individual ratings makes up the score for the
employee.

The graphic, or profile, method lists vertically along the left-
hand side of a chart the characteristics to be evaluated and shows
some appropriate scale horizontally along the top of the chart.
Spot markings opposite the various main characteristics and under
the appropriate place on the scale are joined with straight lines,
thus forming a sort of profile indicating the employee's performance.

The group method lists the characteristics to be evaluated as in
the profile method, but, opposite each character trait to be rated,
specific points are enumerated under four classifications: "superior," "above average," "average," and "below average."

The narrative method provides no set form; it is a general
description of the abilities of the employee, thus fitting the appraisal to the individual instead of including all individuals in
a predetermined scheme for appraisal.

Specimen copies of the above forms are distributed, followed
by a discussion in which general principles for rating are evolved.
These include such matters as considering each characteristic
individually and independently, collecting evidence in support of
the rating, avoiding likes and dislikes, avoiding grades uniformly
high or low, basing ratings over observations covering a period
of time, and so on. The leader points out that improvement can
take place only if the employee is informed of his rating from
time to time. This is a task of counseling, already considered in
the preceding session.

Twelfth Session

The farther up the ladder of managerial authority one climbs,
the more time is spent in conferences. This time can be spent
effectively, or it can be wasted, depending upon the leadership
exercised. There is not much point in a conference wholly domi-
nated by the leader except as a vehicle for communication, nor is
a conference without effective leadership likely to be productive.
The leader should exercise control in introducing the topic and

guiding the discussion, but the group should participate, should have some authority over the decision, and should feel satisfied with the outcome.

The subject of the present session having thus been introduced, the question arises as to whether or not some basic plan applicable to all conferences can be evolved. Four charts are now displayed, labeled, "approach," "drawing out," "acceptance," and "summation," and the group is asked to fill in the details. Under "approach," purpose, scope, and procedure are suggested; under "drawing out," getting facts and opinions and asking pertinent questions are considered important; under "acceptance," the group feels that cross discussion should be spirited and the leader's viewpoint challenged if desired, that all ideas should be evaluated, combinations of ideas considered, and, finally, some conclusion drawn. In the summary it is felt that the leader should emphasize those points in which there is general acceptance, state the action to be taken, if any, and explain the issues left unresolved.

A special conference technique involves the use of questions. They may be directed to a particular individual to start a discussion, or may be placed before the conference as a whole to stimulate thinking. Sometimes a question referred back to the one posing it is effective and will clinch an important point, or possibly a question by one member asked of another may stimulate the expression of opinion.

Another special problem is the handling of troublesome situations, and the group is asked to name difficulties that commonly arise in conference meetings. Control is sometimes difficult, it is suggested; the discussion may stray away from the subject, or maybe the group just remains silent. Perhaps one member is troublesome, or hostility may develop. At this point a sheet which suggests remedies is distributed. These remedies are compared with the difficulties listed, and their possible effectiveness is discussed.

Thirteenth Session

The first session of this course emphasized self-analysis. In this last session the leader directs the attention of the group to self-improvement. A successful executive, he points out, must have the ability to think logically and to express himself clearly. He must be able to lead others and must develop for himself a philosophy of life that justifies achievement and engenders motivation to that end. Would a systematic plan help achieve such a goal? Suggestions for such a plan are made by the group and outlined on the board.

As mentioned in the first session, self-analysis is Step 1. A paper containing suggestions for this procedure is now distributed. This, it is explained, is a personal matter and hence is for private study. It calls for an analysis of interests, aptitudes, and mental and physical health, and an appraisal of intelligence and knowledge. It is suggested that Step 2 might be the defining of both a short- and a long-term goal. (At this point the leader explains the educational program carried on by the company.) Step 3 consists of procedures for meeting these goals. Step 4 concentrates on the present job—the development of both mechanical skills and skills in dealing with others.

A sense of urgency permeates the sessions thus recounted. At one moment the men are in the factory facing problems, hearing complaints, adjusting difficulties, explaining, instructing, and smoothing out maladjustments as best they can. The next moment they are in the classroom, listening to the experience of their co-workers, discussing and analyzing counterparts of the very situations that they faced a moment ago and will face again a moment hence. Under the guidance of an experienced instructor, they hear constructive criticism, are given helpful suggestions, and learn of new techniques constantly emerging from study and research. This is vital education indeed, a blending of learning, applying, reporting, and relearning that plumbs the very depths of reality on the one hand and, on the other, reaches out for the new and improved as revealed by experiment and research. No artificial motivation is necessary; the daily work life supplies it. And no distant use of knowledge gained need be envisaged; it will probably be needed that very afternoon.

VI *A Course in Human Relations*

The study of human relations is today an integral part of managerial and supervisory development. So important has the subject become, however, that it is customarily treated as a separate course of instruction. Its place in industry was firmly established by Elton Mayo (1880–1949) who conducted exhaustive experiments at the Hawthorne Works of the Western Electric Company, Inc., for a period of 12 years (1927–1939). Previously, Frederick W. Taylor (1856–1915), the generally acknowledged originator of scientific management, had taken industry to task for its haphazard methods of production. Centering attention upon the individual worker, Taylor demonstrated how systematic work organization could increase productivity. This emphasis upon the worker may be said to have paved the way for Mayo, but, whereas Taylor concentrated on time and motion, Mayo studied thoughts and feelings,[1] showing correlations with productivity quite as striking as anything developed by Taylor. To Mayo's original findings, much has since been added by industrial psychologists, training experts, and others to make up the subject matter now customarily presented in corporation educational courses on human relations, and described in this chapter.

Although graphic materials, motion pictures, slides, and case studies, explained in the last chapter, are extensively employed, the most progressive teaching methods emphasize specially de-

[1] Georges Friedmann, *Industrial Society,* Free Press, Glencoe, Ill., 1955, p. 313.

vised role-playing techniques which make of the classroom a living laboratory. Situations are created wherein individuals actually experience the thoughts, emotions, and feelings formally explained or discussed at the instigation of the instructor, and it is through these experiences that learning takes place. Conventional subject matter divisions are ignored. Instead, collective and individual tasks are performed involving, perhaps, many of the concepts once considered separately. Data regarding the resulting experiences are then collected and the group made cognizant of their significance.

The ideas instilled in the group through such procedure are outlined in the following pages, the subject matter divisions being inserted merely to facilitate the exposition.

Studying Human Relations[2]

Causes of Human Behavior

Human behavior is the result of some cause or causes. The origins are usually complex, arising either within or without the individual, and the same cause may affect different individuals in diverse ways, influencing their behavior either directly or indirectly through thoughts and feelings. Individuals seldom know why they act as they do, but if their behavior is to be influenced, the reasons must be discovered. This is the task of a good supervisor. He does not treat symptoms but ferrets out the reasons for them, and then focuses his attention upon these reasons. Imputing blame hastily and thoughtlessly makes it difficult to discover the reasons for a particular act because accusation merely prompts defense. Before administering censure, therefore, it is well to try and discover all the relevant facts, or as many of them as possible,

[2] American Telephone and Telegraph Co., New York. The course is called "Personal Factors in Management," its objectives being: (a) to help the supervisor understand himself and how he relates to others, (b) to help him develop more accurate foresight with regard to human behavior, (c) to help him achieve the ability to learn from his own experiences—not just in the training situation, but on the daily job, (d) to help him diagnose situations involving people, i.e., to be sensitive to a wide range of cause-result sequences, and (e) to help him deal with behavior change.

relating to any offense committed by an employee. Then remedial action can be directed to the cause or causes.

Individual Differences

Effective supervision depends in large measure upon noting individual differences and in appreciating their significance in job situations. Some are obvious, such as physical appearance, and, to a certain extent, acuteness of sight, hearing, touch, and so on. Others are less easily noticed and must be discovered by close observation, specially designed tests, or both. Among the latter are motor differences such as finger dexterity, eye-hand co-ordination, and speed reaction, and mental differences, or intelligence, manifested in ability to learn, remember, and reason. Personality differences such as honesty, dominance, persistence, and variations in the will to do, or motivation, are also important.

Individuals are different, it seems, not because they possess different abilities and traits but because they possess the same abilities and traits in different proportions. Records of any measurable ability, obtained from a large number of persons selected at random, show a distribution characteristic of a bell-shaped symmetrical curve—a few with very high scores, a few with very low scores, and a large number with varying scores in between the two. The fact that there are so many different kinds of abilities, and that the range of any one is so great, makes the chances of any two individuals being precisely alike quite impossible.

Individual differences are due to heredity, growth, and learning. Differences due to heredity and growth are innate and are fixed at maturity. They include differences in sensory acuteness and motor and mental differences. Differences due to learning are acquired and are subject to change throughout life. They determine to what extent the innate abilities are utilized.

Performance and Abilities

Performance depends upon a combination of innate and acquired abilities. But in any given job situation, an individual seldom performs up to the full extent of his capacity. This is because job performance includes factors other than ability. High motivation, for example, may increase the production of those with less than average ability, while lack of motivation may decrease the production of those with more than average ability. No matter how high the average production is raised, there will always be some workers who, for want of ability, will produce less than the average, while there will be others, with superior ability, who will produce more than the average. Superior ability is likely to be overlooked, particularly when performance is low. Productivity can usually be increased by training those below average and motivating those above average.

In organizing a work team, the best work group is made up of persons with not too wide a range in ability. Otherwise those with low ability become discouraged, while those with superior ability lack motivation. Individuals lacking the minimum abilities for a work situation are particularly disturbing to a work team.

Motor abilities show little interrelation. Finger dexterity, for example, may be manifested in one job but found lacking in another that would seem to be similar. Poor performance by a worker on one job, requiring high motor skill, is no indication, therefore, that the same worker will not perform well in another job not unlike the first. It should be noted also that motor abilities show little correlation with mental abilities.

Development Through Training

Wide differences exist in the extent to which workers can develop through training. Those with low mental ability can respond only to a limited extent; in fact, practice in such cases may even prove detrimental by fixing existing faults all the more firmly. In general, the more intelligent learn more quickly and easily, remember what they have learned more readily, and apply it with greater facility. The higher the intelligence, the shorter the training period necessary; the higher the motivation, the more rapid the learning. Those with high mental capacity, however, are likely to find a repetitive job monotonous and are not easily motivated under such conditions. Intelligence requirements should be given careful consideration in making placements and transfers, because job satisfaction is at its maximum when the capacity and the personality of the worker correspond with the requirements of the job.

Motivation

When an employee is motivated, some kind of incentive that is outside of himself satisfies or relieves some particular inner need. In large measure motives determine behavior. To understand the behavior of a worker, therefore, it is necessary to know his motives. His motives and hence his behavior can then be influenced through incentives. An incentive may be positive or negative. If it attracts, it is positive and encourages a repetition of the resulting behavior. Reward is a positive incentive. If an incentive repels, it is negative, and while it may stimulate a negative response, it may result in unwanted behavior such an absenteeism. Harsh criticism or punishment are cases in point. Both positive and negative incentives are necessary in supervision, but positive incentives are more conducive to a co-operative work force.

Motives may conflict and have an adverse effect upon job behavior. Perhaps an employee is confronted with a choice between two equally rewarding goals, or between two equally undesirable alternatives, or a single goal may involve both attractive and undesirable elements. The supervisor can often help relieve such conflicts by adding something to the desirable side or deducting something undesirable, and thus induce a satisfying decision.

Individual Goals

Motives determine goals to which every individual aspires. The goal may be less than the possible accomplishments, in which case the individual is satisfied with performance below his potential capacity. Or the goal may be higher than the possible accomplishment, causing the individual constant discouragement and frustration. Ideally, a goal within the range of possible accomplishment, but somewhat above actual achievement, will provide a maximum of satisfaction by making activities attractive and by stimulating development.

Goals are influenced by various conditions. For example, competition may raise the goal level when abilities are reasonably equal, but may reduce it, at least for less capable persons, if abilities are too unequal. Likewise, group performance may raise goals by social pressure brought to bear upon the laggards. When an individual's goal affects the job situation adversely, the supervisor can often institute remedial measures. For example, if the worker's goal is unrealistic, subgoals may be devised, nearer his level of accomplishment but a step toward the main goal. Or if his goal is too low, motives may be stimulated by sufficiently attractive incentives. Then again, goals can often be changed to the worker's advantage. The supervisor may induce him seriously to compare his abilities with his achievements and then, through appropriate incentives, influence him to set goals in keeping with his capacity.

Solving the Problem of Frustration

When an attempt to attain a goal is blocked, a problem develops. Efforts are made to overcome the obstacle; if successful, the problem is solved and the next problem to appear may be all the easier for one's having overcome the first difficulty. In this way, personal development takes place. But when efforts to overcome an obstacle fail, the individual often becomes frustrated, and troublesome behavior may develop, affecting adversely his job performance. How serious the maladjustment is depends upon circumstances. Emotionally stable people are less susceptible to frustrations. The greater the number of possible solutions that can be devised, the less likely it is that the problem will appear unsurmountable. Or, if the goal is of little importance, it can be ignored, or a substitute goal, more attainable, can be substituted.

But if the problem is not solved, thrust aside, or replaced, the individual is likely to react in any number of troublesome ways characteristic of frustration. And to make things more difficult for the supervisor, the reactions seldom offer a clue to the source of the trouble. Hostility may develop, for example, and express itself in back talk, faultfinding, sarcasm, becoming argumentative, spreading rumors, or belittling others. Loafing on the job, quitting work early, causing inconvenience to fellow workers, and adopting an irritable manner are also characteristic expressions of hostility. Even physical abuse of machinery and equipment is not uncommon. On the other hand, the individual, faced with frustration, may just give up entirely, become apathetically irresponsive, and manifest extreme discouragement and lack of confidence. Or frustration may prompt an attempt to escape from the problem entirely by daydreaming, resignation, or transfer. Even illness may develop, genuine enough to the individual, but without organic cause. Then again, frustration is commonly recognized by excuses in which blame is placed upon trivial causes or upon others. At times, frustration will manifest itself in regression, meaning that the worker reverts to earlier and less mature methods of handling his work. Finally, there is the possibility of fixation when the individual repeats over and over again some unsuccessful solution to the problem that is troubling him.

Work situations are cited as a fertile source of frustrations, since employees must submit to necessary restrictions and at the same time accede to demands which are more or less exacting. Of the innumerable blockages that may cause frustrations, some are of common occurrence. Desire for economic security is blocked when expected earnings are not realized. The need for emotional security is frustrated by too frequent criticism, failure to keep an employee informed of his progress, insufficient or improper training, or appearance of favoritism. The drive for recognition is thwarted when the efforts of employees go unnoticed, when their suggestions are ignored, or when they are not made aware of their contributions to the general objective of the company. The desire for self-expression is hindered by too monotonous work for long periods of time, lack of opportunities for self-development, or overdomination by supervisors. The need for self-respect is blocked when discipline prohibits reasonable freedom on the job, or when individuals are not treated with consideration or fairness.

Threats and arguments, even appeals to reason, are of little avail in relieving frustrations. Sometimes a barrier can be removed or reduced, as in resolving a conflict or adjusting unrealistic goals. Extra attention can be given to the emotionally insecure person who is disliked or feels inferior, appropriate training can be provided the less proficient, and particular care can be exercised in assigning new and transferred employees to the work best suited to them. Always a tolerant, objective, and helpful attitude is necessary.

Understanding Workers' Attitudes

The Hawthorne experiments, mentioned earlier in this chapter, correlated favorable work attitudes with productivity, an attitude being a predisposition to react in a characteristic manner. Favorable work attitudes were found to exist when managerial policy was consistent with the motives of the work force. Attitudes and motives therefore are closely related. Attitudes, in fact, may well signify motives and hence the behavior to be expected; thus they can serve a useful purpose to the supervisor if they are properly understood.

Attitudes are acquired through experience and learning. Cumulative experiences gained over a long period of time will develop attitudes in keeping with those experiences; a general manager and a factory worker may react very differently to the same situation because of widely divergent individual experiences. Occasions of strong emotional appeal tend to establish attitudes firmly. Attitudes may be taken over ready-made from other people, hence the importance of a supervisor's attitude toward the company. First impressions often create lasting attitudes; witness how proper orientation reduces turnover, as described in a previous chapter. Experiences, of course, do not affect all persons alike, nor do they always impress the same person with equal force. Moods, temperaments, and emotions, as well as sex, vocational occupation, and geographical location must be considered.

Attitudes influence how events are interpreted, what beliefs are held, and the selection of particular elements that appear significant in a situation. Observed facts are colored by previous experience and learning; ideas are accepted or rejected on the basis of preconceived notions, and the things anticipated in a new situation depend upon likes and dislikes already acquired. There is always a tendency to make what is received through the senses consistent with established attitudes.

Likewise, behavior is usually consistent with attitudes, even though the behavior appears illogical to another person. A policy may be accepted because of its logical appeal but may be actuated indifferently because of some hidden feeling. A case in point is that of a supervisor with attitudes conditioned on production, commending one employee for his ingenuity in devising a new timesaving method but reprimanding another employee for infraction of regulations because his new method did not happen to work. An irrational decision, arrived at impulsively, may be perfectly consistent with long-established attitudes. Certain duties may be postponed and certain people avoided when logical procedure would dictate otherwise. In a sense, people always behave logically, but it is often necessary to understand their attitudes to appreciate the logic.

Attitudes vary in their amenability to change. Those recently acquired are flexible; those of long standing, however, or associated with strong emotional feelings or deeply established frustrations, are highly resistant. The fact that attitudes are acquired, however, suggests that new ones can be developed through new experiences and learning. Changing an employee's work situation, for example, may often accomplish the desired result, and the fact that the satisfaction of motives tends to inculcate favorable attitudes opens the way for making substitutions. Informing an employee of impending changes that otherwise might be disturbing to his motive for personal security often helps, since people usually react unfavorably to situations that they do not understand. Then again, since attitudes frequently are associated with emotions, they can often be changed through an emotional appeal, however trivial, such as a small accommodation, a friendly word, or a helpful suggestion. Individual counseling is usually effective if wisely conducted, and there are advantages in working through individuals even when group attitudes are a problem. Apart from the group, each individual's attitudes can be considered separately without danger of their being strengthened by the presence of others who are like-minded. On the other hand, sometimes when an employee expresses an attitude before a group, it does not sound nearly so convincing as when justified in solitude, and if the group once begins to change, individuals support one another in effecting the altered point of view. Many supervisors find that a combination of individual counseling and group discussions can be used to advantage. In any case, favorable attitudes are such a valuable asset to a work force that efforts to create them are infinitely worth while.

Counseling

Much can be learned about people by observing them, analyzing their work, and hearing what others say about them. But for effective understanding, it is necessary to talk with them. Besides the informal day-to-day contacts, supervisors are called upon to interview employees when engaging them, instructing them, hearing their grievances, correcting their faults, reviewing their progress, assisting in personal adjustments, and when employment is terminated. Such interviews may be helpful or harmful in building morale, depending upon the methods used and the skill of the interviewer. No longer, however, are results left to chance. Principles established by long experience and painstaking study are followed. These do not assure success but greatly increase its possibilities. Supervisors can short-cut the long, and often precarious, process of learning by trial and error if they know and apply these principles.

Differences in status create a natural barrier when a supervisor interviews an employee, but this can be overcome to a great extent. The supervisor can at least avoid argument, cross examination, or lecturing which will only raise the barrier by forcing the employee to fight back in defense of his self-respect. And on the positive side, to help establish accord, mutual interests can usually be developed out of the problem at hand. The employee should be made the central figure in the interview by being encouraged to express his views freely, and by patient listening on the part of the supervisor. Whatever is said should be considered important. The task of the supervisor is to remain objective, conscious of his own biases and prejudices. If confidential information is imparted, it should be held inviolate unless permission is granted to pass it along to other authorities. The employee should be encouraged to arrive at his own conclusions, particularly if a personal problem is involved, advice being confined to furnishing information which may not be known to the employee. A friendly relationship established by such means will go far toward reducing interferences that hinder mutual understanding.

Of all the techniques found effective in interviewing, none is more difficult to apply than that of listening. Those in managerial capacities are accustomed to giving orders. It is understandable, therefore, that the first inclination on the part of the supervisor should be to tell what is what, ignoring any viewpoint on the matter held by the employee, and assuming that he will share in the one expressed. But if a genuine desire is created on the part of the supervisor to understand the employee, the habit of listening will follow naturally. And by listening, much can be learned, for ofttimes what is said is not an objective statement of fact but a reflection of motives and attitudes that may be revealing. Nor is it generally difficult to get the employee to talk. An encouraging manner such as a nod of the head, a smile, or just a pause will help, a short neutral response in which interest and understanding are expressed, or simply a repetition of the last remark or phrase uttered by the employee will often help keep the flow of talk alive. Questions should be used sparingly, as they may guide the employee away from expressing his true feelings, but if they are necessary, they should be phrased in such a manner as to encourage further expression. "Yes" and "no" answers seldom reveal the true story. By thus being encouraged to talk, the employee develops a better understanding of himself, and, by listening, the supervisor gains a surer base on which to support any necessary action, and a more certain evaluation of how that action will be received.

This understanding-listening approach requires practice under actual conditions, and the supervisor will do well to check his technique until habits become firmly established. An "I said—he said" verbatim account might be written up after each interview and checked with the principles learned in this course. Marginal notes of omissions and commissions can then be made, preparatory to subsequent improvement.

Importance of Group Attitudes

Thus far the subject matter has considered only individuals, their personal aspirations, problems, motives, attitudes, and behavior characteristics. But people at work are not isolated individuals. They are members of groups. Some of these groups are established by virtue of the corporation organization for the purpose of determining lines of authority, facilitating operations, and providing paths of communication. Then again, there are groups within groups, and groups composed of members of various other groups. These develop without formal planning. They may be based on friendship, antagonisms, type of work, status, or any one of many other mutual interests. But however groups are formed, the individuals composing them are influenced by one another, and many of their motives are satisfied only through their membership and participation in the group as a whole.

Often a few individuals will form a small exclusive group. Sometimes a group will divide into several smaller groups. Frequently, two persons will form a friendship. Often, one person will remain apart, not accepted by the others, and in nearly every group certain individuals will be popular with almost everyone.

Such relationships present supervisors with problems as well as opportunities. News, rumors, gossip, and complaints circulate through subgroups. Perhaps an improved method of keeping individuals currently informed would check this tendency. A small exclusive subgroup indicates a lack of unity and low morale, perhaps ineffective leadership. The rejected person is a problem, especially as he is likely to develop troublesome behavior, therefore measures designed to develop his self-confidence and to bring him into group activities are called for. When several subgroupings are formed, conflict may develop, especially when the weaker group becomes powerful enough to challenge the stronger one. Development of common aims and objectives should be attempted. The popular individual, and probably a natural leader, can be a hindrance to the supervisor, but he can also be a help in developing morale and changing attitudes. And dual friendships usually make good working partners. Supervisors can uncover such relationships by close observation and by making it a point to know each individual personally.

The group exerts a strong influence upon the individual. His motives being satisfied in large measure through the group, he is sensitive to what is thought and said, or by what he assumes to be thought and said. But this social pressure is not resented, as a rule, because it applies to all members of the group alike, and the individual himself has a part in formulating it. When practices, actions, and decisions are accepted and approved by the group, therefore, the enforcement is automatic, but when rejected by the group, the burden falls entirely upon the supervisor.

People generally have just as much capacity for co-operation as they have for conflict; whether one or the other predominates will largely depend upon the supervisor. If he succeeds in engendering a sense of participation and a feeling among members of the group that they have a personal and definite part in the group activities and a share in the determination of procedures, their motives will be satisfied, their attitudes constructive, and their behavior co-operative.

Communication

A free flow of information throughout an entire organization is a vital necessity for the development of co-operative groups. Communication from the top down makes for unity, engenders a sense of belonging, and builds morale. Communication from the bottom up helps management formulate policies in consideration of the motives and attitudes of the employees and gives the employees a sense of importance because they are heard and their viewpoints are considered. Downward communication may be blocked by misinterpretations, lack of time to pass along information, or disregarding information of no personal interest. Supervisors should realize that matters which seem trivial to them may be of interest to their subordinates when relating to their jobs. Upward communication may be hindered by a tendency to ignore bad news, by a reluctance to pass on information that may be detrimental to a supervisor and his relations with the group, or by an indisposition on the part of those in upper management to listen. But if each one in authority insists upon good communication within the area of his own jurisdiction, effective over-all communication will be assured.

Leadership Authority

Leadership is based upon authority. One sort of authority comes from the corporation as a part of the job. Another kind comes from the group and is the result of the association of the leader with his subordinates. The first kind is formal and automatic; the second must be earned. It is earned by appealing successfully to the motives of the workers. If these motives are satisfied through the total job situation, employees will work together co-operatively and effectively and will willingly accord authority to their leader.

Leadership authority may be exercised in different ways, three different types being customarily recognized, but no one of the three is used alone. First there is the dominating type in which the authority vested in the leader by the corporation is supreme and the group is little more than a reflection of his thinking and planning. He supervises closely, and his subordinates display little initiative, assume little responsibility, and enjoy scant opportunities for development and growth. The group may react with resentment or submission, depending upon the manner and skill of the leader in exercising his authority. This method is relatively easy, requiring little resourcefulness.

Then there is the *laissez-faire* way of exercising authority. It is characterized by a lack of leadership, activities of the group being determined largely by the members themselves. Disagreements, bickerings, and confusion are common, and results are poor. A degree of *laissez faire* is sometimes useful, however, in developing self-reliance, in permitting some individual to escape from difficulties, or when delay is advisable for some good reason.

Finally, there is the democratic approach. Here, reliance is placed largely upon the earned authority of the leader. He is an active participant in the activities of the group. Morale is high, and results are good, because most of the job motives of the workers are satisfied. Initiative, assumption of authority, and wide opportunity for personal development are present. This is the most effective method for creating a spirit of co-operation and a desire on the part of individual workers to apply themselves to the job at hand. But it is the most difficult method to develop, requiring a high degree of understanding and resourcefulness. Although all three of these types will be used by the effective leader, it is the democratic method that, by engendering a sense of participation, develops and maintains the characteristics most desired in a working force; that is, the will to do a good job, and a certain flexibility and readiness to meet changing conditions so essential in industry today.

Regardless of the methods used, certain personal characteristics are prerequisite to effective leadership. There must exist a liking for people, for the leader must work with them co-operatively, understand them, and be accepted by them. Emotional stability is required in constantly making adjustments to different personalities and varying situations. The leader must possess self-confidence, since those having this trait are more likely to encourage new ideas and suggestions, develop subordinates, and welcome problems as a challenge to their abilities. It is important that leaders possess a sensitivity to others, because attitudes must be known but are seldom obvious. An effective leader will realize that it is his job to get along with the group and to engender co-operation, interest, and enthusiasm within the group because it is the group that will get the work done. Persons aspiring to leadership must have all of these qualities to some extent at the outset, but from that point on they can be developed and expanded by study, practice, self-analysis, and the gradual formation of habits that assure skill in handling the multitudinous situations that arise every day in job situations.

Perhaps many of the ideas and ideals set forth in the above body of subject matter are more often violated than practiced, but the very fact that they are being taught by such an overwhelming number of the largest corporations in the country is significant.

A culture lag commonly exists before practices catch up with ideas, but, in this case, events are conspiring to reduce the interval in any such lag. Some say that it is the scarcity of man power that is inspiring a revolutionary change in labor relations; others claim that it is the workers themselves, who, having gained much in wage demands, are now insisting on more nonfinancial satisfactions: still others point out that industry, having succeeded in supplying at least the minimum of the necessities of life, is devoting more attention to spiritual values.[3] No doubt all of these factors are playing their parts, but two other circumstances of paramount importance should not be overlooked. Ethical codes have preached human co-operation from time immemorial, but research and experimentation in the social sciences are now disclosing just how that co-operation can be accomplished. And, since Elton Mayo's Hawthorne experiments, industry has been shown that education in the principles and methods involved pays good dividends.

---

[3] Eugene Staley (Ed.), *Creating an Industrial Civilization, a Report on the Corning Conference,* Harper & Brothers, New York, 1952, p. 27.

Engineers, chemists, metallurgists, and other technically trained graduates come to business usually well-grounded in the basic knowledge pertaining to their several professions, but they cannot be expected to know all the details of every specialized industry that may require their services. If a career in business machines is chosen, the graduate will probably not be versed in all the details involved in the design and production of analog computers, the principles of circuit logic, or the techniques of electric-computer design. If it is the airplane industry that he plans to enter, he will probably have to learn something about fusilage construction, collective pitch throttle synchronization, and drive-train systems. Or, if contemplating the petroleum industry and confronted with a modern fluid catalytic cracking unit with its sixteen stories and three acres of pipes, valves, furnaces, vessels, pumps, and controls, he could hardly be expected to know very much about the practical operation of such a monstrosity. Unlike the managerial and supervisory courses, the subject matter he must learn varies widely from industry to industry. He must master a specialty within a specialty.

That specialization has proceeded apace ever since the days of Adam Smith's pin factory is common knowledge. That specialization has now reached the point where technical institutions of higher learning can no longer cope with it, is, perhaps, less widely understood. In aeronautics, computing-machine engineering, electrical, chemical, and many extractive industries, to mention only a few examples, new knowledge and revolutionary techniques are accumulating with bewildering rapidity. So rapid is the pace, in fact, that no one institution can possibly hope to offer all the advanced courses necessary adequately to prepare graduates for original scientific research and advanced technical work in all the varied industries undergoing such kaleidoscopic development. The administrative problem alone would be baffling; the financial investment in laboratories and machines necessary for such a wide range of highly specialized teaching would be prohibitive, especially when such equipment can, through obsolescence, become valueless almost overnight. Advanced technical education conducted by industry, therefore, is no encroachment upon the prerogatives of the conventional technical institutions. It is an activity superimposed upon the existing educational structure by necessity, and a development that can well be regarded as an inevitable consequence of cumulative knowledge and the ceaseless march of minute specialization.

The paragraphs that follow outline a few courses of instruction offered by corporations to engineers and other technical graduates to prepare them for research and other highly specialized work in specific industries. Some of these courses occupy 100 hours, many from 60 to 70 hours, others between 30 and 40 hours. The descriptions will probably not be very meaningful to readers lacking technical training and experience. Many persons have the notion, however, that educational activities conducted by industry are of rather an elementary if not superficial nature. A glance at the pages immediately following will, it is believed, dispel any such impression.

Electronic Computer Circuit Design

A qualitative and quantitative design course in four related areas of study. Emphasis is given to component tolerances and economics; reliability, serviceability. Part 1. Rapid review. Basic definitions, laws, theorems; circuit transient analysis; electron tube theory; Laplace transforms, Fourier analysis. Problem solving with supervision. Part 2. Digital pulse circuit design. Computer tube types and characteristics; inverter, cathode follower, oscillator, tree-running multivibrator, flip-flop, univibrator, blocking oscillator, phantastron, gating, squaring, clamping and scaling circuits; diode switching circuits, gas tube circuits. Part 3. Transistor theory and circuit design. Semiconductor physics, equivalent circuits, transistor types and characteristics, load lines; grounded configurations; amplifiers; inverter, emitter follower, multivibrator, flip-flop, logical switching circuits. Recent transistor component and circuit development. Part 4. Magnetic theory, materials and circuit applications. Core types and characteristics, multi-dimensional core memory systems, logical circuits. Recent developments and applications of magnetic components.

Electronics Laboratory and Instrumentation

Theory and application of instruments used in engineering laboratory. Instrumentation errors; component tolerances and effects. Tube, semiconductor and magnetic circuits included. Emphasis on use of oscilloscope, transistor and magnetic components.

Principles of Computer Electronics

A descriptive course in basic electronics as applied to computer circuits. Review of fundamentals of electricity and electron theory. RCL circuits; basic tube types and characteristics, basic computer circuit configurations and their characteristics (tubes, transistor and magnetic component circuits); fundamentals of circuit logic and logical block diagrams; circuit wiring diagrams.

Principles of Circuit Logic

Formal and intuitive approach to functional circuit design. Boolian algebra, relay and diode switching, coding, translating and converting; decimal, binary and coded-decimal adders, accumulators; miscellaneous circuits. Emphasis on logic rather than component. Lecture, discussion, practice exercises.

Machine Design Analysis and Application

Design of machine components for proper performance. Topics: strength of materials, vibration and dynamics, impact analysis; cam, gear, clutch and spring design, package and assembly design; tolerances; statistical dimensioning. Consideration given to reliability, serviceability and human engineering factors.

Experimental Mechanical Measurements and Instrumentation

Introduction to practices and techniques employed in measuring quantities associated with mechanical-electromechanical devices. The use of transducers combined with appropriate instruments employed in a resistive, capacitive, magnetic, piezoelectric, photoelectric, thermoelectric, electronic and radioactive manner; high-speed movies.

Electronic Packaging Practices

Introduction to engineering, manufacturing, testing and assembly specifications. Components, pluggable units, chassis layouts, fabrication, mounting and cooling; printed wiring, printed circuits; connectors and cables.

Computer Principles

A general, descriptive course related to historical development, philosophy, logical organization, characteristics, and layout of input, output, arithmetic, storage and control sections of computing systems. Survey of analog computers and servomechanisms; recent developments, future organization of digital computers.

Student Seminar[1]

This course is conducted by a class seminar chairman elected by the group participating. The chairman works with the instructor in the selection of seminar topics and the scheduling of seminar meetings. Each class member prepares and presents two 15-to-20-minute technical papers. Topics are approved by the instructor and a copy of the speaker's notes in outline or abstract form is submitted to the class seminar chairman at least 3 days in advance of the presentation. The use of visual aids is encouraged. Each presentation is constructively criticized by class members. Criticism is directed anonymously in writing to the speaker. Also, a tape recording is made of the presentation for the student's personal evaluation. Thus the speaker benefits by a realization of his faults of organizing, delivery, etc. and can take steps necessary to improve.

Creative Engineering

Introduction to basic techniques to illustrate how the review of one's knowledge of fundamentals of engineering and science can provide the challenge to combined acquired knowledge with present needs to arrive at new developments for the future.

[1] Information furnished through the courtesy of the International Business Machines Corporation, New York.

Experimental Aerodynamics

This course is being presented to provide an understanding of the factors involved in producing experimental results. Topics include: concepts of similarity and the use of models, wind tunnel nomenclature, description of the various wind tunnel types, wind tunnel design, corrections, flow visualization, instrumentation, survey of standard testing and data analysis procedures.

Aerodynamic Flight Test

The basic theory of flight airspeed and altitude, techniques of data measurement and reduction, determination of static and dynamic flying qualities, performance measurement, thrust determination, and flight test techniques employed to isolate and eliminate deficiencies in flying characteristics.

Seaplane Design

Review of hydrostatic and hydrodynamic principles, nomenclature, and past designs of water-based aircraft. Development of hull proportions and detailed design parameters. Evaluation of model test results for resistance, stability, spray, and water loads. Application of skis and hydrofoils to seaplane designs.

Advanced Propulsion

Concepts involved in the technical aspects of propulsion work. Application of theory, working data and curves which are utilized in obtaining the solution to many problems confronting the propulsion engineer. Review of the elements of thermodynamics and gas dynamics and application to propulsion problems. Induction system design problems for both subsonic and supersonic flight; performance of jet engine components; and methods of presenting and treating jet engine performance.

Advanced Aircraft Performance

Theoretical and empirical background for drag estimation of modern aircraft. Incompressible boundary layer theory and supersonic wave drag estimation. The Navier-Stokes equations will be derived and particular solutions will be obtained. Laminar and turbulent boundary layer characteristics. The supersonic area rule will be derived and detailed applications shown.

Heat Transfer

Heat transfer as applied to aircraft practice. Steady and unsteady state conduction; free and forced convection; heat transfer at high velocities; fin theory; heat exchanger design; radiation; boiling and condensing.

Advanced Engineering Mathematics Review

Complex numbers, de Moivre's theorem, determinants, logarithms and exponentials, plane and solid analytic geometry, transcendental functions, limits, and continuity, differentiation and integration, differential equations, vectors, Couchy Riemann equations, Fourier series.

Theory of Elastic Stability

Buckling, lateral buckling, beam column, second and fourth order differential equations for buckling, buckling for single span rod, solutions for pinned pin and fixed pinned, elastic curve of fixed-free columns, energy method of buckling, finite difference methods or any end conditions, stepped column, plates and cylinders under end loads, shear loads and normal loads.

Introduction to Nuclear Technology[2]

A survey of the nuclear engineering field at a graduate level. Emphasis will be placed on the engineering aspects without subjecting the student to rigorous mathematical derivations. The following topics will be covered: atomic structure, nuclear physics, uranium and thorium ores, radiation hazards and detection, shielding, health physics, reactor theory and types, separation of isotopes, spent fuel reprocessing, applications.

[2] Glenn L. Martin Company, Baltimore, Md., *Evening Education,* 1956–1957.

VIII *General Education*

Of the 296 corporations reporting educational activities of some kind, only 47 indicated having a program in general education. Where such programs are offered, however, they are generally extensive, include a wide variety of subject matter, enroll hundreds and sometimes thousands of employee students, and are housed in buildings devoted exclusively to education. One company contracted with a leading university to co-operate in the establishment of its program. For 5 years and at a cost of over $100,000 in services, the university and the corporation worked together in formulating objectives, developing instructional materials, and measuring educational achievement. A number of doctoral dissertations have resulted from the project. What is taught in its off-hour program is determined by the employees themselves, with subjects ranging from blueprint reading to foreign languages, economics, and psychology. Many of the courses are open to the wives and children of employees. There is no tuition charge, and textbooks are loaned.[1] Another company reports offering some 1,500 separate courses with an enrollment of 32,000 employees (1956). Its annual expenditure for educational purposes amounts to between $35,000,000 and $40,000,000.[2]

In order to give some idea of the scope and nature of these general educational programs, the present chapter presents the

[1] International Harvester Company, Chicago, *Adult Education in Industry,* a brochure, not dated.

[2] Information furnished through the courtesy of the General Electric Company, New York.

subject in three sections[3] and in increasing detail. First, the variety of subjects offered is shown in a consolidated index listing the titles of 446 separate courses offered by 6 corporations. Second, brief over-all descriptions of three general educational programs are presented. Third, certain courses are described in detail. Two of these, rapid reading and creative thinking, have been selected because of their unusual character, their growing popularity, and the high functional value imputed to them by those who have succeeded in mastering their contents. A third subject, economics, has been selected for detailed consideration because of its general interest to businessmen and to show the nature of the subject matter selected for presentation by one representative company.

Consolidated Index of Courses[4]

Avocational Subjects

Bridge
  Beginners
  Intermediate
  Advanced
Ceramics
Charcoal Sketching
Current Events
Dancing
  Beginners
  Advanced
Gardening
Golf for Beginners
Good Grooming
Home Maintenance and Repair
Interior Decorating

[3] Below and pp. 97 and 99.

[4] Courses listed (by titles) offered by 6 out of 47 corporations reporting a program in general education. Exact titles of courses offered by 2 or more corporations are not repeated, but similar titles are listed because of the emphasis often indicated by the wording. Dan River Mills, Incorporated, Danville, Va.; General Shoe Corporation, Nashville, Tenn.; International Business Machines Corporation, New York; Johnson & Johnson, New Brunswick, N.J.; Glenn L. Martin Company, Baltimore, Md.; and Socony Mobil Oil Company, Inc., New York.

Oil Painting
Photography
Sewing
Woodworking

Business Machines

Accounting Machine Applications
Accounting Machine Practice
Analog Computer Techniques
Application of Digital Computers to Engineering and Industry
Central Computer
Data Processing System
Digital Computers
Digital Computers and Problem-programing Procedures
Electronic Data Processing Machine
Introduction to Programing
Linear Programing
Network Analysis
Principles of Data Processing
Principles of Stored Program Computers
Pulse Techniques and Circuits
Scientific Programing
Theory of Programing
Transients in Linear Systems

Communication

Communication in Business and Industry
Communications
Employees Communication Practice

Economics

A.B.C. of Economics
American Business System
Business Economics
Business Economics for Executives
Common Stock, What Is It?
Corporate Procedures and Practices
Economics for Everybody
Industrial Economics

Investment Principles
Personal Finance

Elementary-school Subjects

Arithmetic
English
Penmanship
Reading
Spelling
Writing

Engineering—Aeronautical

Advanced Aircraft Performance
Advanced Gas Dynamics
  Part I
  Part II
Advanced Propulsion
Advanced Stability and Control
Aerodynamic Flight Testing
Aerodynamics
Aircraft Flutter and Transient Loads
Analytical Methods for New Design
Experimental Aerodynamics
Fundamentals of Engineering Aerodynamics
Heat Transfer
Hydrodynamics
Seaplane Design
Unsteady Aerodynamics

Engineering—Electrical

Applied Electronics
Basic Electricity
Basic Electronics
Basic Principles of Electronics
Correlation of Transient and Frequency Responses
Electrical Measurements
Electrical Navigation Aids
Electrical Practice
Electricity, Elementary
Electronic Circuit Analysis
Electronic Circuits

Electronic Packaging
Electronics
  Elementary
  Advanced
Elementary Electrical Circuits
Elements of Electrical Engineering
Engineering Electronics
Engineering Principles of Electronic Data Processing Machines
Industrial Electronics
Introduction to Transistors
Laplace Transform Methods for Electronic Engineers
Magnetic Core Circuits
Oscilloscope Applications
Pulse Circuits
R.F. Measurements
Servomechanisms
Switching Circuits Logic
Transistor Applications
Transistor Theory and Circuits

Engineering—Mechanical

Advanced Airloads
Advanced Feedback Control Theory
Aircraft Vibrations
Bonding Techniques and Processes
Elementary Strength of Materials
Elementary Structural Aerodynamics
Engineering Mechanics
Engineering Statistics
Experimental Metallurgy Laboratory Techniques
Fundamentals of Heat Transfer and Thermodynamics
Fundamentals of Tool and Die Design
Kinematics
Lube and Allied Products Course for Experienced Engineers
Mechanical Drawing
Mechanical Systems
Metallurgy
  Elementary
  Advanced

Plastics Engineering
Principles of Machine Shop Practice
  Elementary
  Advanced
Principles of Mechanical Design
Production Illustration
Sintered Metals
Strength of Materials
Theory of Elastic Stability
Tool Design Drawing

Engineering—Miscellaneous Subjects

Business and Legal Aspects of Engineering
Engineering Forum
Engineering Report Writing
Industrial Engineering
Product Engineering and Manufacturing
Slide Rule Practices

High-school Subjects

Algebra
American Government
American History
Basic Mathematics
Biology
General Chemistry
General Science
English
Plain Geometry

Human Relations and Psychology

Basic Psychology for Supervisors
Business Psychology
Creative Thinking
Human Relations
Human Relations Applied to Salesmanship
  Elementary
  Advanced
Human Relations Conference
Human Relations in Supervision

Improving Teamwork
Practical Psychology
Psychology in Human Relations
Selected Problems in Human Relation.

Managerial and Supervisory

Conference Techniques
   Conference Leadership
   Getting Results from Group Meetings
   Meeting Leadership
   Planning and Holding Group Meetings
Controls
   Control of Labor Costs
   Cost Accounting
   Cost Estimating
   Cost Improvement
   Emergency First Aid Squad Training
   Fire Fighting
   First Aid
      Elementary
      Advanced
   Manufacturing Control
   Methods, Time-Measurement
   Quality Control
   Quality Control Supervisor Training
   Safety
   Safety Pays
   Safety Practices
   Scheduling and Production Control
   Waste Control
Internal and External Relations
   Employee Relations
   Job Relations Training
   Personnel Management for Supervisors
   Public Relations
   Public Relations, Principles and Services
   Standard Personnel Practices
   Survey in Employee Relations
Interviewing and Counseling
   Counseling

Employment Interviewing
Interviewing Technique
Managerial Development
Attitudes and Supervision
Be a Better Supervisor
Business Management, Principles of
Case Studies in Management
Effective Management
Fundamentals of Management
Management Development
Manufacturing Division, Management Development Program
Manufacturing Trainee Program
Organization and Management Conference
Organization and Management Refresher
Personal Development
Personal Efficiency
Standards of Business Conduct for Management
Traffic and Transportation
Production
Effective Job Organization
Foreman's Responsibilities
Grievance Procedure
Job Evaluation
Job Methods
Job Methods Training
Labor Analysis
Merit Rating
Organization of Work
Performance Rating Program
Preparation and Conduct of Grievances
Technical Training
Time Study and Wage Incentives
Transportation and Packaging
Union Contract Administration
Union Contract Interpretation
Wage Incentives
Work Improvement
Work Simplification
Public Speaking
Dale Carnegie Course in Public Speaking

Effective Presentations
Effective Speaking
  Elementary
  Intermediate
  Advanced
Effective Speech
Practice in Effective Speaking
Public Speaking
Rapid Reading
  Improve Your Reading
  Reading, an Approach to Writing
  Reading Improvement
  Reading Program
  Speed Reading
  Speed Reading and Comprehension
Teaching
  Audio-Visual Aids Workshop
  How to Instruct
  Job Instruction Training
  Lesson Instructing
  Quality Control Inspector Training
  Quality Control Supervisor Training
Writing
  Effective Writing
  How to Write Clearly
  Memo and Report Writing
  Report Writing
  The Editor's Workshop

Manufacturing and Production

General
  Assembly Planning
    Elementary
    Advanced
  Blueprint Reading
  Electrical Practice
  Fitting Department
  Hand Cutting
  Job Methods
  Machine Shop Planning

Machine Shop Practice
Manufacturing Processes
Manufacturing Training Program
Mechanical Drawing and Blueprint Reading
Metal Cutting Tools
Pipe Fitting and Plumbing
Precision Measurements
Principles of Automation
Sheet Metal Planning
Shop Applications of Mathematics
Slide Rule Practice
Statistical Quality Control
   Elementary
   Advanced
Stores Operation
Warehousing (Storage)
Welding
Welding Planning
Petroleum
  Bunker Oil
  Crude and Wholesale Products
  Light Products Basic Training
  Petroleum Loss Control
  Specific Light Products Course
  Traffic Management in the Petroleum Industry
Textile
  Automatic Box Loom Fixing
  Automatic Plain Loom Fixing
  Automatic Spooler and High Speed Warper Fixing
  Bleach House Processes, Operating and Maintenance
  Card Fixing and Grinding
  Chemical Finishing Operations
  Cloth Analysis and Design
  Cloth Construction and Analysis for Finishing Mill
  Color Matching
  Comber Fixing
  Dobby Head Fixing
  Drawing Frame Fixing
  Drawing Room Operations and Sewing Machine Adjustment
  Drawtex Fixing

Dyeing Processes, Operating and Maintenance
Fly Frame Fixing
Inspection Put Up
Instrumentation
Nonautomatic Spooler and Low Speed Warper Fixing
Opener, Cleaner, and Picker Fixing
Physical Finishing Machinery, Operation and Maintenance
Ply Yarn and Cord Analysis
Related Chemistry and Dyeing
Sewing Room Operations and Sewing Machine Adjustment
Textile Manufacturing and Nomenclature
Textile Testing
Try-in Machine Fixing
Twister Fixing
Winder Fixing

Mathematics

General
  Advanced Engineering Mathematics Review
  Algebra
    Intermediate
    Advanced
  Arithmetic Systems and Devices
  Basic Mathematics
  Calculus
  College Mathematics
  Differential Equations
  Digital Logic
  Elementary Statistics
  Geometry
    Plane and Solid
    Analytical
  Introductory Calculus
  Laplace Transform Techniques
  Linear Equations and Matrices
  Mathematics Review for Engineers
  Matrix Algebra
  Nomography
  Nonlinear Equations
  Numerical Methods

Pre-engineering Mathematics
Probability and Game Theory
Quality Control Applications
Statistical Quality Control
Trigonometry
Textile
Advanced Finishing Mill Mathematics
Bleachery Calculations
Card Calculations
Drawing Frame Calculations
Elementary Yarn and Cotton Mill Mathematics
Fancy Cloth Calculations
Finishing Mill Mathematics
Finishing Mill Mechanical Calculations
Fly Frame Calculations
Intermediate Yarn and Cotton Mill Calculations
Loom Calculations
Mechanical Calculations
Open, Cleaner, and Picker Calculations
Plain Cloth Calculations
Ply Yarn Calculations
Ribbon Lapper and Comber Calculations
Roving and Yarn Calculations
Silver Lapper (Lap Winder) Calculations
Slasher Calculations
Slide Rule Calculations
Spinning Frame Calculations
Twist Calculations
Twister, Spooler, and Warper Calculations

Office Subjects

Accounting, General
Business Law
Business Letter Writing
Clerical Records
Comptometer Calculations
Elementary
Advanced
Credit Organization and Administration
Domestic Purchasing

Effective Letter Writing
English Review
Everyday Law
Export Purchasing
Government Contract Law and Practices
Office Administration, Principles of
Office Practices
Secretarial Practices
Secretarial Training
Shorthand
  Elementary
  Advanced
Shorthand, Alphabetic
Shorthand, Gregg
Shorthand and Typing Brush-Up
Supervisory Problems in the Office
Telephone Practice for Employees
Timekeeping
Traffic Management
Typewriting
  Elementary
  Advanced

Orientation

Annual Report Presentation
Background Course
Company Organization and Operations
Credit Policy
Familiarity Program, Service Department
Financial Policy
History of the Company
Know Your Company
  Preliminary
  Tours
Laboratory Observation Tours
New Employee Introduction
Orientation
  All Employees
  Key Employees
Orientation, Advanced

Plant Informational Program
Product Informational Program
Products
Purchasing Policy
Refinery Information and Observation Tours
Review of Home Office and Domestic Field Accounting
    and Financial Policies, Practices, Procedures
Sales Policy
Service Department Familiarity Program
Standards Department

Physics and Chemistry

Advanced Nuclear Technology
Basic Principles of Chemistry
College Physics
General Physics
Introduction to Nuclear Technology
Kinematic Analysis
Modern Physics
Nuclear Reactor Engineering
Physical Chemistry
Physics Review
Polymer Chemistry
Practical Physics
Radiation Hazards and Health Physics
Radioisotopes Techniques
Solid State Physics
Survey of Chemical Structure
Transistor Physics

Research

Leadership Training for Research Personnel
Operations Research Survey
Research Problems
Research Symposium

Sales Subjects

Advertising
Advertising and Sales Promotion
Aviation Marketing

Bulletin Writing for Sales Executives and Division Managers
Course for New Salesmen and Engineers
Diagnostic Sales Training
Distribution
Distribution Analysis
Industrial Marketing Course
Introduction to Export Traffic
Marine Sales
Market Research
Marketing Analysis
Marketing Engineering
More Results Methods
Principles and Methods of Sales and Supervision
Retail Factors and Advanced Study
Retail Merchandising
Retail New Development Training
Retail Operations
Retail Products Training
Retail Sales and Service and Service Station Experience
Retail Training Course for New Instructors
Sales Manager Training
Salesmanship

General Programs

High-school Courses Included

One corporation[5] offers 111 separate courses. There are 2 semesters a year of either 10 or 16 weeks each, depending upon the subject. Special classes are organized during the summer as needs dictate. Classes meet twice a week, usually from 1 to 3 P.M. or from 7 to 9 P.M. to accommodate both day and night shifts. With a few exceptions, classes are held on the time of the employee. Some classes are restricted to employees, others are open not only to the families of employees but to the public as well. Instructors are chosen from qualified employees when possible, otherwise are engaged on a part-time basis. Tuition is charged for all classes,

[5] Dan River Mills, Incorporated, Danville, Va., Training Department, *Dan River Evening Training Program, Course Catalogue. Everything from A to Z,* typewritten.

varying from $2.50 to $6.00 per student. Upon completion of a course, the student receives a credit card, and a permanent record is made in the training department. Of the 111 courses offered, 60 are technical and apply to the industry of which the company is a part, 23 are supervisory and managerial development courses of a general nature, 13 are clerical courses, and 15 cover academic subjects. The academic courses include 2 in public-school subjects and 13 in high-school subjects. Upon completion of the high-school subjects, a student is graduated and receives a diploma, fully approved by the city and state boards of education.

On Company Time

Another company[6] offers 53 courses varying in duration from 1 day to 12 weeks. All courses are given during the day on company time and are open to all employees. Instructors are either full-time teachers attached to the training department or company personnel engaged for part-time instruction. There is no charge. Of the 53 courses offered, about half are technical and concerned with the company's industry and product, and about half are of a general business nature.

A third company[7] offers 47 courses, each comprising from 3 to 12 sessions of 1½ hours each, held during the day on company time. Instructors are drawn from the training division as full-time teachers, or from operating departments of the factory on a part-time basis. There are no tuition charges. Of the 47 courses offered, 21 have to do with the company product, 16 are general courses on business subjects, and 10 have to do with avocational or culture interests.

A Graded Program

This company[8] offers 90 courses. The classes meet for a 2-hour period once a week for 12 weeks during early evening or after-

[6] Socony Mobil Oil Company, Inc., New York, *1956 Calendar of Employee Development Courses.*

[7] Johnson & Johnson, New Brunswick, N.J., *Training Catalogue,* Jan. 15, 1956.

[8] Information furnished through the courtesy of the International Business Machines Corporation, New York.

noon hours. Instructors are drawn both from the company personnel and from school and college faculties on a part-time basis. There are no tuition charges, and textbooks are loaned. Of the 90 courses, 12 have to do specifically with the company's product, 58 are of a technical nature, 10 are clerical, and 10 are general cultural subjects. The program is arranged so as to enable students to progress from elementary levels up to college and graduate standards in the more advanced courses.

Specific Courses

Rapid Reading

In one corporation[9] an informal survey, conducted among its executives and supervisors, disclosed that they spent on an average of from 4 to 5 hours a day reading, including the time spent both in and out of business. Tests showed that those who participated in the course on reading improvement started with an average reading speed of 243 words a minute and a comprehension score of 65 per cent. Subsequent tests at the end of the course indicated that the average reading speed had advanced to 459 words per minute with no decrease in comprehension. Several individuals, who started at about 220 words a minute, moved up to 600, with a comprehension of 70 per cent. One person started at 214 and finished at 970 with a comprehension of 80 per cent. Another, who started at 543 and a comprehension of 65 per cent, increased his speed to 1,144 and his comprehension to 90 per cent.

Nearly every business executive is confronted daily with an endless stream of letters and reports, and, in addition, has to read numerous periodicals and books to keep abreast of his particular interests, to say nothing of the reading he would like to do for recreation and pleasure but for which he probably cannot find the time. Here, then, is a fruitful source of timesaving, and in this corporation many of the executives considered it worth while to devote an hour or so twice a week for 18 weeks to save hours of time every day thereafter.

[9] Johnson & Johnson, New Brunswick, N.J., Training Department, *Reading Improvement Training,* revised 1953, typewritten.

Each session begins with a 7- or 8-minute film. The film contains reading material, only one phrase or group of words of which is in focus at a time. The rest is blurred and unreadable. The phrase or group of words at first in focus then becomes blurred, while a second group appears clear and readable. Then the second group goes out of focus and a third group becomes readable, and so on throughout the entire passage. There are 16 such films. The time that the readable words remain in focus is gradually reduced in each film from the second to the sixteenth, and there are successively fewer word groupings per line. The first film calls for a reading speed of 180 words per minute, and there are five in-focus groupings per line. Later films require a reading speed of 470 words per minute and there are only two groupings per line. Thus, from session to session, the participants gradually learn to step up their reading speed by observing more words at a time and requiring less time for each observation.

Following the showing of the films, the participants are given a comprehension test consisting of 10 multiple-choice questions. The tests are then scored, and the questions and answers are discussed. Mature students will not accept an answer as correct just because it is so marked on the instructor's master key. Analysis of some questions is desirable, therefore, and a satisfactory explanation of why only one of the alternate answers is considered a correct one must be given.

The progressive nature of the series of films makes it essential that no class sessions be missed. This is difficult with busy executives. Different sections, of from 15 to 20 participants each, meet on different days and at different hours. If a student misses his regular session, therefore, he can attend the session of some other group covering the material that he missed. Even so, it is necessary to provide some means whereby a participant who is unable to attend any section for a period of time can keep up with his class.

This is accomplished by means of another mechanical device known as an "accelerator." It consists of a rack that supports the reading material over which there is a movable shutter. The shutter can be adjusted at any predetermined speed, and the reader must keep pace with its movement down the page as the upper part of the reading material becomes covered. The speed of the shutter is adjusted to correspond with that of the reading films missed, and the student thus maintains his rate of progress along with his regular class.

The class, now having completed the reading film and its appropriate comprehension test with everyone satisfied as to the accuracy of the answers, is given individual reading passages of two or three pages. At a given signal all begin to read, each his own material. The instructor indicates the elapsed time on the blackboard every 10 seconds. When a student finishes his assignment, he refers to the blackboard, notes the time that it has required him to complete it, and proceeds to a comprehension test based on the material just read. The final scores for speed and comprehension for both these selected readings and the reading films are kept by the student. These records, it is said, create a good deal of interest as progress is noted. Participants can be seen comparing them during lunch hours and at other odd times during the day.

At the end of each class session, an optional period of 15 minutes is given to vocabulary building. Individual counseling and diagnostic tests sometimes reveal that lack of comprehension is due to a limited vocabulary. Technical personnel will often have an extensive vocabulary applicable to their particular specialty, but a relatively small one otherwise. A standard textbook is used in this part of the work, two chapters being covered at each session.

In addition to these regular features of each class session, various special skills and helpful knowledge contributing to increased reading speed and greater comprehension are considered from session to session. For example, the participants are asked to read short magazine articles and to summarize the main theme in a brief statement. Practice is given in recognizing paragraph development, key words, and transitional phrases, and in skimming to grasp quickly the main ideas developed by an author. Impediments to rapid reading, such as vocalization and regression or the habit of going back over lines already read, are pointed out. The significance of eye movements and the span of vision are discussed, and physical and psychological defects are explained.

Occasionally, a third mechanical device may be used. This is the "tachistoscope" or "flash meter." Its purpose is to increase the participant's ability to distinguish symbols in a given observation. Numbers are first used, then words, then short phrases, and, finally, longer phrases. The symbols are flashed on a screen for a predetermined length of time, the intervals being reduced and the number of symbols increased as the student becomes more proficient. Thus, help is given in reducing the time necessary to read a group of words and in increasing the number of words that can be grasped at a single observation. The tachistoscope supplements the reading film and the "accelerator."

An interesting supplementary activity to encourage practice between class sessions was devised by the teaching staff. A brief reading exercise, timed to reach the participants in their morning mail, provides a review of some phase of the course just covered. Perhaps the recipient is asked to skim the passage and then answer two or three factual questions pertaining to it, timing himself while doing so. Or, for practice in anticipation, he may be asked to read rapidly part of a brief story and then to fill in the blank lines at the end indicating what he thinks should be the outcome. Such mailing pieces are usually given close attention and stimulate interesting discussions at the next class session.

This course in reading improvement has now been offered for a sufficient length of time to justify some tentative conclusions as to its merit. After an interval of 3 years, over half of those who participated in the first course were tested. Of these, 50 per cent were found to be reading even more rapidly than they had at the completion of the course, and all were reading more rapidly than they had at the beginning of the course. Analysis of the group's comprehension ability showed an increase of 63 per cent per reading minute. Collectively, the group started the course reading 226 words per minute; at its completion the score was 403 words per minute. The retest showed a speed of 392 words per minute. The teaching staff feels that the results indicate a definite lasting value, although categorical conclusions are reserved pending additional group retesting.

Creative Thinking[10]

People can be trained to think up new ideas, according to a convincing body of empirical evidence. Under various titles such as Applied Creative Thinking, Applied Imagination, Creative Imagination, Creative Problem Solving, Creative Thinking, and others, such training is being given in many of the leading corporations as well as universities and technical institutions. In a company, 500 students graduated from a course of this kind in 1955.[11] In another, 1,400 students completed such training in 1956.[12] Of the 10 largest corporations in the country, 9 offer this sort of instruction in one form or another.[13] In 1955, a company reported that 400 graduates of its creative-engineering program developed new processes and patentable ideas at an average rate nearly three times that of its nongraduates.[14] Another company has authorized the statement that after 12 sessions the students showed an average improvement of 79 per cent[15] in their flow of ideas. Others report similar results.

The point is advanced that, of the two main kinds of thinking, judicial and creative, the former constitutes a large part of formal education and grows automatically with experience, while the latter is neglected and atrophies with nonuse. Tests indicate that creative talent, however complicated its composition may be, is like other mental traits, normally distributed. Its effectiveness, however, depends more upon the mental energy applied to it than to inborn capacity. While it is doubtful, therefore, that innate creative capacity can be increased through training, there is every

[10] This material has been drawn largely from Alex F. Osborn, *Applied Imagination, Principles and Practices of Creative Thinking,* rev ed., Charles Scribner's Sons, New York, 1957, and other literature supplied through the courtesy of the Creative Education Foundation.

[11] General Motors Corporation (*The Third Year,* a pamphlet published by the Creative Education Foundation).

[12] United States Steel Corporation, Gary plant (*Ibid.*).

[13] General Motors Corporation Standard Oil Company (New Jersey), Ford Motor Company, United States Steel Corporation, Chrysler Corporation, General Electric Company, Swift & Company, Bethlehem Steel Corporation, Armour & Company (*Ibid.*).

[14] General Electric Company (*Ibid.*).

[15] National Cash Register Company (*Ibid.*).

reason to believe that its effectiveness can be, and experience seems to support this conclusion.

Just how this can be accomplished most effectively has been the subject of a large amount of study, research, and experimentation inspired by Alex F. Osborn, who started pioneering in this area during the 1930's. Since then, much has been added through experience. In 1954, Osborn established the Creative Education Foundation. With variations, of course, the principles and practices recommended in the literature published by this organization form the basis of most current instruction in the subject.

The instruction consists of textbook material and exercises. The one is helpful in understanding mental processes, the other essential in convincing the student of his latent creative abilities and in developing those abilities through use. The more theoretical part of the instruction calls attention, for example, to certain blocks to creative thinking. Critical judgment is one of the most serious. All ideas must eventually be evaluated, of course, but the separation of creative from judicial thinking is advised. First comes "free wheeling"; think of all the ideas possible, whether practical or impractical, possible or impossible, sensible or silly. The first objective is quantity; quality can be judged later. Other blocks are more or less subsidiary to this one. Avoid fixation, meaning long-established habits of problem solving. Search for a new approach. Timidity is as fatal to creative thinking as is conformity. Don't hesitate to appear foolish; the ideas may turn out to be good ones after all; many "foolish" ideas have done so. Self-discouragement is also a serious block. Concentrate hard. If the yield is meager, take a rest and try again. Some kinds of imagination are automatic, daydreaming for example, but not creative imagination. This calls for conscious effort.

Likewise, procedures that encourage creative imagination are presented. Break up the problem into specific targets; frame it in the form of a question, and write it down. A question clearly stated is half answered. The richer the background of experience, either firsthand from personal observation or vicarious from reading and study, the better the results. This is because idea associations reach back into memory and then spring forward in imagination to produce new ideas. Even games that call for some sort of creative exercise, and recreational activity that requires ingenuity, can help limber up the mind for creative thinking.

The exercises include questions relating to the text material and problems designed to stimulate creative thought. For example, "How can the problem of downtown parking be solved?" Or, "How can more citizens be induced to vote?" These and similar problems may be assigned for individual consideration in between class periods or for group creative thinking during the class session. In one class, about 10 minutes are devoted to introductory explanations by the instructor; 20 minutes to questions, answers, and discussions based on the text material; about 45 minutes to a problem, first listing the ideas suggested for its solution, then evaluating the results; and, finally, 10 minutes are given to summarizing and about 5 minutes to explaining the next assignment. From 13 to 15 such seminars are recommended. As might be expected, training consists for the most part in practice, for, just as practice can increase proficiency in mental traits, so can it increase the effectiveness of creative thinking.

Emphasis is placed on the point that there is no formula for the creative process, no set procedure. Certain steps are mentioned, however, to call attention to essential phases in creative imagination. Orientation states the problem; preparation assembles the essential information; analysis breaks down the total problem into its constituent parts, defining specific targets; incubation provides rest periods, permitting budding ideas to formulate; synthesis combines ideas, improving those already made; and, finally, judicial thinking separates the usable from the unusable.

Individual creative thinking is essential, particularly in original research where each researcher must be permitted to register his own creations and carry them through to conclusions. Many times, however, collaboration is mutually stimulating and more productive. When two persons join together for creative thinking, it is recommended that each devote a certain amount of time to individual effort and that they then meet at intervals for dual creative thinking or evaluation. Creative thinking in groups larger than two has been dubbed "brain-storming." Here the source of individual ideas is waived in favor of a common pool. It is said to be the most productive plan for generating ideas, since one thought suggests another as individual members of the group are stimulated by one another's contributions.

Certain special procedures, born of experience, are recommended for "brain-storming" sessions. For example, the optimum number has been found to be 12: 5 are pace setters, persons who have been found to be particularly fluent in suggestions; 5 are guests selected for their knowledge of the problem to be posed, and they are expected to participate actively; in addition, there are a leader and an associate leader, preferably individuals who have been trained in the techniques of group creative thinking. It is desirable that the participants all be of about the same rank in the hierarchy of business. A record is made of all ideas presented, a tape recorder sometimes being used for this purpose. Four rules must be observed explicitly:

(1) There must be no criticism of any idea presented; the leader has a bell at his side which he rings any time this rule is violated.

(2) Inhibitions must be overpowered. Any idea at all is welcome; evaluation is another and later process.

(3) Improvements on ideas already proposed are encouraged. It is recommended that the participants be notified of the problem the day before so as to provide a period of incubation.

(4) No written memoranda are permitted. The session must be spontaneous, informal, and conducted in a spirit of fun. A post-session is desirable, perhaps the next day, or one conducted by written memoranda, thus giving participants an opportunity to record any afterthoughts that may have occurred to them.

Osborn reports that in one organization, 46 groups conducted 300 creative-imagination sessions during 1955. The total yield was 15,000 suggestions, 1,000 of which proved worthy of development. As a general rule, about 10 per cent of the ideas generated are usable. It is recommended that screening for these usable ideas be conducted by a second group composed of individuals selected for their judicial proficiency, objectivity, and judgment as to what is feasible.

Economics

Unlike the subject matter presented in the two examples cited above, that presented in economics is more informational than functional. No training in skill is involved unless it be skill in good citizenship, sharpened by increased knowledge of economic life. Furthermore, the subject is not, in this particular corporation plant, presented as a separate course of instruction. Individual economic topics are considered frequently in regular weekly meetings of supervisors where various subjects, some relating to the more technical aspects of the business and others to affairs of a more general nature, are discussed. Each economic topic, therefore, is a unit in itself. There is no sequential development and no dependence on one topic for an understanding of another. Each topic is presented in an attractive pamphlet, simple in style and profusely illustrated with meaningful charts and interesting pictures. Five of these pamphlets are summarized here to give an idea of the subject matter presented.

Our Dynamic Economy

The dynamic nature of the economy provides an interesting topic. Why, it is asked, has the national economy surged forward with few interruptions for more than 150 years? There are other nations with valuable natural resources, healthful climate, and capable scientists, and some with more land area and people, yet almost half the world's supply of goods and services is produced in the United States. A provable answer is probably impossible. More effective use of the factors of production has certainly contributed to this success, however, and many hold an abiding faith that the freedom enjoyed by individuals in satisfying their economic needs, administering their political affairs, determining their own vocations, and enjoying the right to acquire private property and to govern their individual lives is a basic cause.

Progress is shown in figures by the total market value of the final goods and services produced, called the gross national product, and by the national income obtained by subtracting indirect business taxes and depreciation allowances from the gross national product. Even allowing for price increases, real output has nearly doubled since 1939. This is reflected in an increase per capita of disposable income from $1,055 in 1939 to $1,540 in 1953. Family incomes have increased sharply, particularly in the lower- and middle-income groups.

Productivity is the key to progress. To date, it has increased at the average rate of about 2 per cent per year. Vast capital investments, increasing from about 4½ billion dollars in 1939 to 25½ billion dollars in 1952, rich natural resources, and an alert and willing work force have made this possible. In the past, many feared that increased productivity would create unemployment, but today it is generally agreed that job opportunities increased and hours of work decreased with stepped-up productivity.

A stable economy depends upon balancing production with demand. To this end, management must predict what, and how much, consumers want. This is a difficult task, since wants are constantly shifting for various reasons, and over-all spending, saving, and borrowing tendencies change from time to time.

Production once determined, the competitive price system acts as an automatic means of distributing goods and services. Individuals receive income on the basis of their contributions to the economy. They spend it in accordance with their wants and desires, and productive enterprise, in turn, converts natural resources into goods and services to meet consumer demand.

All of this suggests a continuous exchange of goods and services on a vast scale. Money makes this possible. The Federal Reserve System regulates the money supplied through its control of bank reserves and interest rates and its policy in buying and selling government securities.

Profit indicates efficiency in meeting competition. A profitable enterprise can pay good wages, provide job security, produce more and better products, and pay its owners sufficient to warrant the risks involved. It can also provide research facilities for creating new products and improving old ones, and can create new facilities for expanding markets, all of which means additional job opportunities. Unprofitable operations will, in the long run, usually force inefficient producers out of business, while high profits will attract new producers, thus increasing competition and stimulating increased efficiency.

It is management's job to maintain efficiency in production, to provide for distribution, and to keep these operations abreast of the constant changes in the economy. At the same time, consumers, owners, employees, and even the general public must be kept satisfied, since industry today is very conscious of its responsibilities to the community and the nation.

All of these involved relationships go to make up a competitive economy. Everyone competes in some way or another throughout life. But along with competition there is co-operation, since everyone benefits. Business competition is the most powerful stimulant yet devised for assuring the continuous progress of the economy.

Inflation

Another topic considered is that of inflation. What if all prices were suddenly deflated to their 1939 level? Savings accumulated over the years would then buy a lot more than they will buy today. On the other hand, a house purchased 10 or 12 years ago would not be worth nearly so much in dollars and cents. There are advantages and disadvantages in inflation, depending upon individual circumstances.

Inflation is caused by buyers trying to purchase more goods and services than are being produced. Demand then exceeds the supply; buyers bid against one another for the available supply, and this causes prices to advance. When the demand and supply of goods and services are in balance, the general price level remains constant.

Monetary and fiscal policies pursued by the Federal Reserve System and the government aim at keeping the general price level constant. But this is not always possible. During war periods, for example, the government must borrow from the banks to meet increased expenses. It exchanges government bonds for expendable funds. This increases the money supply, which is immediately spent for the needed goods and services to carry on the war. Demand increases, but the supply of goods and services cannot be increased as rapidly. Prices therefore advance.

The supply of money more than trebled from 1939 to 1952. During the war, consumer spending was curtailed, but government spending more than made up for it. After the war, many consumers reduced their savings to satisfy pent-up demands, other bought on the installment plan, business concerns replaced worn-out equipment, residential construction precipitated an enormous demand for various commodities, and many foreign governments sought American products. All of these forces combined to increase the demand for goods and services beyond the ability of productive enterprise to produce; hence the great rise in prices.

This increase in the money supply was reflected in an increase in disposable personal incomes which climbed from 70.2 billion dollars in 1939 to 235.0 billion dollars in 1952. But this does not mean, of course, that consumers could purchase more than three times the amount of goods and services. The price advance made it necessary for them to pay more for what they did purchase. However, the average hourly earnings of some workers increased even more than the general price level. For example, the average hourly earnings in one industry advanced from 93 cents in 1939 to $2.03 in 1952. Deducting "inflation" from the $2.03, the amount becomes $1.06. Even so, these particular workers could buy somewhat more in 1952 than they could in 1939, despite inflation.

Workers in most manufacturing industries have fared pretty well during this period of inflation, but others have suffered. Those who have had all of their savings in bank deposits and savings bonds have sacrificed purchasing power. People living on fixed incomes, such as pensions and social security, have had to reduce their living standards. Teachers, policemen, firemen, and others whose salaries increase but slowly and seldom adequately are in much the same position.

Inflation depends ultimately upon the American people. Their votes determine what public policies are pursued by the government, and their buying decisions shape the forces that create or check inflation. Uncontrolled purchasing power, when prices are rising, will make further advances all the more likely. Every postponed purchase at such a time helps to check the upward trend.

The Business Cycle

Discussing the business cycle, it is pointed out that a perfect cycle is a theoretical conception beginning and ending in a trough. It starts at a low point, then proceeds upward by way of recovery and prosperity until a boom period develops, then gradually declines through a recession and depression until another trough is reached. But this does not always happen. Boom times may not develop into a depression. A brief recession may be followed by prosperity. There are peaks and valleys but seldom a clear-cut beginning and end to a business cycle.

Today there are indications that the high crests and deep troughs, which have characterized the dynamic development of the economy, can be reduced. But the very nature of the economy, emphasizing as it does freedom of individual decisions and actions, encourages sudden changes, resulting in great surges forward during which maladjustments accumulate, and to correct these requires periods of quiescence. The very facts of freedom and growth make some fluctuations necessary.

One of the main causes of fluctuations in business activity today is the variation of investments. When incomes are high, spending is free. Producers, operating at capacity, are then inclined to expand their facilities not only just enough to supply the current demand, but somewhat more, in anticipation of a still larger volume of purchasing. On the other hand, if buying levels off, producers are likely to anticipate a decline and postpone all expansion for the time being. Thus a slight change in consumer spending can affect a material change in investment policy.

Investment policy, in turn, affects consumer spending. The construction of new machinery, buildings, and equipment causes money to be paid out for wages. Some of this is saved, but most is spent. If spent for consumer goods, the department stores and other retail establishments become active, with high payrolls. Their employees save some of their wages but spend the greater part. This process is repeated again and again. Thus a relatively small investment pyramids into a considerable amount of consumer purchasing.

Investments thus stimulate and, in turn, are stimulated by consumer spending. The first is called the multiplier principle, the second the acceleration principle. Applying these principles, it is easy to see how changes in investments may precipitate a recession or stimulate a boom. If consumer spending tapers off, investments are postponed. This cuts into consumer income. Spending is decreased, and more investments are postponed. If this process goes far enough, there may not be sufficient economic activity to absorb all the labor force. Recession, and perhaps depression, develop. But if consumers spend freely, investments are encouraged, incomes are increased, and still more spending occurs. A boom period follows. Indeed, this may be carried so far that the demand for goods and services exceeds the ability of producers to supply it. The boom then develops into an inflationary trend.

If a trend in economic activity could be anticipated, planning of business and government activities would be greatly facilitated. But forecasting is still a matter largely of interpretation and judgment. Statistics, however, are the basis of all such evaluations. One set of figures, widely used, assumes that different areas of the economy move in about the same sequence as the various stages in the business cycle. There is a leading series consisting of the number of business failures, the wholesale price index, and other factors. This series usually turns down early in a business recession and turns up early in recovery. The coincident series, made up principally of unemployment figures, the gross national product, and industrial production, usually turns up or down a little later than the leading series. And there is a lagging series of which personal incomes, sales of retail stores, and manufacturers' inventories take a leading part. This continues to decline throughout the recovery phase of the business cycle and to keep on advancing until a recession is well under way. These indicators performed in this manner during the 1948 and the 1953–1955 recessions. And they may prove valuable in the future in forecasting trends.

A trend, once discernible and believed to be proceeding beyond a danger point, can be checked to a certain extent. During a down turn in economic activity, the government can reduce taxation, permitting individuals and corporations to retain and spend a larger portion of their incomes. Unemployment compensation, social security, and private pension income, minimum wages, and farm price supports, all help sustain purchasing power. The Federal Reserve System can reduce the interest rate and otherwise make it easier to borrow for investment purposes. And, as a last resort, the government can increase its own spending by various kinds of needed public works. When boom periods get out of hand, taxes can be increased, government spending curtailed, and interest rates advanced to discourage overexpansion and excessive speculation.

After the second quarter of 1953, the gross national product turned downward and continued so until the third quarter of 1954. Reductions were made in excise and personal income taxes, and the excess profits tax was removed. Government payments to individuals, in the form of unemployment compensations, pensions, veterans' benefits, and so on, increased, and there were some advances in wage rates. During the latter part of 1954 a new upturn started. There is good reason to believe that, although progress will not always be without interruptions, depressions need not paralyze economic life.

Taxation

A fourth pamphlet deals with taxation. It points out that in 1952 there were 116,743 different tax-collection units in the United States—the federal government, the 48 states, 67,346 school districts, and 49,348 other local government units. And the tax bill was a big one—79 billion dollars in all. The federal government collected about 60 billion dollars, the state governments 10 billion dollars, and local governments 9 billion dollars. In 1939 the total tax receipts were 10 per cent of the gross national product. In 1951 this percentage had grown to 26 per cent. As taxes grow, problems relating to them multiply.

Everyone wants fair taxation, but just what is fair? Should

taxes be based on what is earned, what is owned, on amounts involved in sales, or something else? Then again, consider the question of apportionment of taxes. Equal payments would make everyone share the tax burden alike. If apportioned on a basis of benefits received, those who are benefited to the greatest extent would pay the most. If based on ability to pay, the wealthy would pay more, regardless of the number of taxpayers or who enjoyed the most benefits. There are elements of fairness and injustice in all of these plans.

Most authorities agree that a fair tax should have the following characteristics: (1) It should be expedient; that is, it should represent the best possible compromise at the time; it should be easily determined, difficult to avoid, the collections should be certain, and the income adequate to meet the expenses anticipated. (2) The tax should be reasonable, meaning that it should not exceed the taxpayer's ability to pay, and should have a favorable effect upon his disposition to engage in productive effort. (3) Whatever taxes are determined upon, they should enjoy public acceptance, otherwise collections are difficult owing to widespread evasion.

Personal income taxes account for about 50 per cent of all the federal budget receipts in 1954. The tax rate ranges from 20 per cent on incomes not over $20,000 to 91 per cent on incomes of over $200,000. It is expedient in that the withholding feature facilitates collection of about two-thirds of the receipts, and the balance is payable in quarterly installments. A short-cut method of calculating the tax is available for income of less than $5,000. It is reasonable because of the ability-to-pay feature, the various deductions permitted, and the fact that very low incomes are virtually tax free. Taxpayer acceptance is good.

Taxes on corporate incomes amounted to about 33 per cent of all the federal tax returns in 1954. About two-thirds of the states levy this tax. It accounted for about 8 per cent of their revenue in 1952. Both the federal government and most of the states impose a flat rate on all corporations, regardless of size. The federal government taxes all corporation incomes at 30 per cent and adds another 22 per cent to incomes over $25,000. Many states set a flat rate of between 2 and 8 per cent. The tax is expedient in that it is easy to collect, difficult to avoid, and the administration expenses are low. But many businessmen hold the view that high corporation taxes reduce incentives to produce and invest, with consequent unfavorable effects on the economy as a whole.

Taxes on real estate are a major source of revenue for local governments. They receive from 85 to 90 per cent of their income from this source. States no longer impose this tax to any extent, receiving less than 4 per cent of their incomes from this levy. The tax may be said to be based on the benefits-received principle. There are wide differences in assessment policis, but otherwise the tax is expedient in that it is easily administered and yields a large and dependable revenue. Opinions differ as to its reasonableness. Some hold that it is unfair because it is not based on ability to pay. Acceptance is generally good, however, because of long tradition and the feeling that property owners benefit the most from the services furnished by local governments.

As a revenue producer, excise and commodity taxes rank second to income taxes. A federal manufacturer's excise tax is levied on certain commodities such as home appliances, business machines, gasoline and automotive products and accessories, and various sports and hobby equipment. The federal government also imposes a retail excise tax on furs, jewelry, luggage, and toilet equipment, and a gross-receipts tax on the sale and transfer of securities. General sales taxes provide a substantial part of the revenues for states, amounting to 23 per cent of their income in 1952, and these taxes provide to a much lesser extent for local governments. These taxes are easily administered and collected; there is little resentment on the part of consumers because small amounts are collected at a time, and these are often hidden in a larger sales price. Then again, many of the excises apply only to luxuries. Objections are often raised, however, because these taxes also violate the ability-to-pay principle, the costs of collection are high, and there must necessarily be product discrimination.

Not only does the question of fairness become a matter of increasing concern as taxes increase; so also does the effect of taxation upon the economy as a whole. For example, a general sales tax tends to reduce consumer demand, an excise tax on manufacturers may advance prices and have the same effect, and taxes on particular items may change buying habits. Taxes on profits may affect a producer's decision to expand his business or may influence others who are contemplating starting new enterprises. And when money collected by the government is spent, there is less consumer sovereignty, since the government, through its purchasing, determines the allocation of natural resources.

Tax policies in a democracy are the ultimate responsibility of the voters. The tax load depends upon the amount of goods and services the government supplies, and this is determined by what the people demand. The kind of taxes that are levied and how they are apportioned are decided by government officials who make their ideas known and then are selected directly or indirectly by the electorate. Intelligent action depends upon an understanding of the tax structure, the problems involved, and a realization that personal welfare is a reflection of the prosperity of the nation as a whole.

Federal Spending

A great deal is being said these days about government spending and the public debt. The gross national product is three and a half times what it was in 1929, but federal spending is forty-five times as great, and the public debt is sixteen times the 1929 figure. Remarkable economic progress has been made during the past quarter century, but federal spending and the public debt need watching.

Most people think immediately of waste, duplication, and other unnecessary expenditures. Even maximum efficiency, however, would not solve the problem. If government spending is to be reduced materially, the voters must say what services they wish curtailed or suspended. This is difficult. The problem becomes apparent when a typical federal-government budget is broken down into governmental functions.

Of the total 65½ billion dollars in the 1955 budget, 63 per cent was allotted to national security. This includes such items as the purchase of military equipment, payments to personnel and operating expenses of the armed forces of the United States, military aid, atomic development, and the stockpiling of strategic and critical materials.

Interest on the public debt accounts for another 10 per cent. The debt is represented by savings bonds held by about 40 per cent of the American families. Banks, insurance companies, and other private institutions as well as government trust funds, all hold large quantities of government securities of various kinds. Nearly all call for interest payments either semiannually or at maturity.

There are now more than 20,000,000 veterans. Together with their families, they constitute 40 per cent of the population. Compensation and pensions to about 3,000,000 of the individuals and families must be paid. In addition, care for the sick and injured and help in rehabilitating others to normal living must be provided. Such expenditures absorbed about 6 per cent of the 1955 budget.

About 3½ per cent of the 1955 budget was accounted for in farm price supports and related programs specified by law. A relatively small proportion of the 3½ per cent was allotted to technical assistance—soil conservation, flood control, expansion of rural telephone services, helping farmers to develop efficient farms, and similar services.

Grants to the states account for most of the 2.8 per cent allotted to social security, welfare, and health. Other expenditures in this category include medical and hospital services, low-cost lunches to 9,000,000 school children, and assistance to 400,000 Indians.

For the development of river basins, construction of power plants, managing millions of acres of national parks and public lands, and for operating 87 fisheries and 275 wild-life refuges, and for research aimed at discovering new uses of mineral products, 1.7 per cent of the 1955 budget was required.

An additional 2.2 per cent consisted of funds granted to the states for the maintenance and additions to the national highway system, funds to provide for operations on oceans and waterways, including such projects as the St. Lawrence Seaway, and funds for air-navigation aids and postal-service operating deficits.

International affairs and finance demanded 1.9 per cent of the budget. More than 80 per cent of this was absorbed by projects providing economic and technical assistance for the development of friendly nations, thus adding to national security.

Government functions, including education and general research, required less than 1 per cent of the budget. And a final 1.8 per cent, or $1,200,000, was absorbed in general government expenses such as salaries to Congressmen and operation of the Weather Bureau.

Of all these allotments, some 90 per cent are fixed expenditures and can be reduced only by changing laws. Expenditures for controllable programs represent only about 10 per cent of the total. The task of reducing materially federal expenditures, therefore, is not an easy one. Even proposed curtailment or abandonment of items in the controllable part of the budget raises many problems.

Equally serious complications arise when a reduction of the public debt is considered. Either taxes must be raised, or government spending must be reduced. It is generally considered unwise to raise taxes during a period of reduced economic activity, because this reduces consumer purchasing and intensifies the recession. Likewise, to retire government bonds owned by commercial banks at such a time reduces bank loans, hampers business, and curtails consumer credit. A national long-range debt-reducing policy would keep taxes high during a period of prosperity and reduce the government spending and the debt. Then, in times of a threatened recession, taxes could be reduced and government spending increased, by borrowing if necessary. But high taxes are not popular at any time, and the voters will have to decide just where to cut government expenditures.

Voters can encourage a sound fiscal policy by becoming familiar with the federal budget, requiring less government service, and insisting that policies be followed that make for a stable economy, thus encouraging continued prosperity and progress.

Co-operation with Formal
Educational Institutions

Thus far, this report has considered only those programs carried on entirely within the jurisdiction of the corporations. As pointed out in Chapter II, a few over a quarter of the companies reporting educational activities limit their programs to this area. Most companies, however, also offer their employees opportunities to continue their education in traditional schools, colleges, and universities. In fact, many make special arrangements with one or more formal educational institutions whereby employee attendance is facilitated. One authority estimates that 100,000 business executives and some 700,000 persons of lower business status are currently attending self-development courses of some kind.[1] No doubt a large number of these receive assistance from the corporations that employ them. To this end, the companies offer various plans, considered in this chapter under three main headings: College Level, Graduate and Undergraduate; Education Below the College Level; and Scholarships, Fellowships, and Loans.

College Level, Graduate and Undergraduate

Company-sponsored educational programs at the college level generally follow four over-all patterns: (1) courses offered on the company premises; (2) courses held on the college campus but attended exclusively or mainly by company personnel; (3) a

[1] *Wall Street Journal*, Sept. 11, 1956, p. 1, quoting Lawrence A. Appley, President of the American Management Association.

co-operative arrangement whereby the student employee alternates between the college campus and the company plant, spending a period of a few months at each; and (4) tuition refunds applied to courses taken at night at local institutions or for an extended period of time under leave of absence spent at some distant college.

In some cases it is possible for a student employee to earn an advanced technical degree without leaving the company premises. The courses offered are wholly within the jurisdiction of some university. Its own teaching staff passes upon admissions, conducts the courses, and administers examinations in accordance with the same regulations and standards that apply on the college campus. Courses successfully completed, in fact, are credited toward work completed in residence. In one company,[2] classes are held after working hours for 2 periods of $1\frac{1}{4}$ hour each, separated by a dinner hour. Normally, a student employee can complete 1 course each semester, or 2 a year. All tuition fees and textbook costs are frequently assumed by the company.

In centers where colleges and universities are not too distant from a company plant and the registration is sufficiently large, special courses on both undergraduate and graduate levels are arranged for company employees. This plan permits of a wide choice of curricula. Degree candidates can follow their chosen majors, or graduates in one field can pursue studies in some related area without degree credit. Engineering and other technically trained personnel, for example, often find it desirable to receive supplementary instruction in business and management courses. The plan offers the added advantage of using company experience in regular course presentations. Half of the tuition is frequently paid by the company, and, for some curricula, the entire tuition is paid. Other expenses such as registration fees, books, and supplies are paid by the student employees.[3]

What is variously known as the co-operative plan, the Cin-

[2] Information furnished through the courtesy of the International Business Machines Corporation, New York.

[3] Westinghouse Electric Corporation, *Continued Education,* Announcement of Courses, 1956–1957.

cinnati plan, or just the work-study program, is becoming increasingly popular among big corporations, technical colleges, and engineering students. Inaugurated at the University of Cincinnati in 1906 with 27 students, by the end of the academic year 1953–1954 the number had grown to over 20,000, or 10 per cent of all the engineering students in the United States. Today the University of Cincinnati's entire engineering program is organized on the co-operative plan, and at least 53 other institutions, including some of the leading technical schools in the country, provide for it to some extent in their curricula. Hundreds of industries from coast to coast co-operate to make the plan possible.[4]

Basically, it provides a study and employment sequence. In some cases students are paired, one working on the job and the other studying on the campus alternate semesters. Thus they jointly hold some one appropriate position. At other institutions the students spend a more prolonged period in industry and likewise at the college. Procedures differ, but generally the plan applies to the last 3 years of a 5-year engineering curriculum. A typical program might require attendance at college during the entire first 2 years. The summer of the second year is then spent in industry. During the third and fourth years, the fall and spring quarters are spent in college, the winter and summer quarters in industry. The fall quarter of the fifth year is spent at college, the winter quarter in industry, and the spring quarter at college again, terminating in graduation. Some institutions permit work experience to begin after the first quarter in college but require continuous attendance at college during the senior year. Instead of 6 practical work periods, as outlined above, other colleges permit only 3; still others allow 12.[5]

The plan was originally conceived as a means of providing a better technical education by combining theoretical college learning with practical industrial experience. Contemporary conditions have multiplied the advantages. With college expenses so high,

[4] *Work Experience Education Programs, American Secondary Schools,* Bulletin No. 5, U.S. Department of Health, Education, and Welfare, Office of Education, Washington, D.C., 1957.

[5] McDonnell Aircraft Corporation, St. Louis, Mo., *The Engineering Student Cooperative Training Program,* a brochure.

the $200 to $275 earned monthly while on the job, often with traveling expenses added, is a matter of concern. For the student, industry serves as a giant laboratory, enabling him to become familiar with equipment that the most highly endowed university could not possibly afford. And for the corporation, a source of man power is supplied that at least provides some advantage at a time when technical talent is so scarce.

The student usually works for the same company during all quarters spent in practical work. Although neither the company nor the student is committed to any permanent employment arrangement, many students are eventually employed on a permanent basis by the company where they have received their training.

During recent years the co-operative plan has been extended to curricula other than engineering. At the University of Cincinnati, the College of Applied Arts is said to offer the only co-operative plan in architecture. At that institution and many others, business administration is included, and a few colleges adapt the plan to the A.B. degree. At least two institutions are said to use the co-operative plan in their graduate schools, but generally the nature of the requirements, even on a second-degree level, makes its application difficult.

In one reported study, in which employers were asked their opinion of co-operatively trained engineers, 56 per cent are said to have reported a favorable opinion; 10 per cent, no difference; 8 per cent of the replies were unfavorable; 25 per cent lacked any experience on which to base an opinion.[6]

The most popular plan for encouraging employees to continue their formal education is through tuition refunds. Indeed, this might be said to be almost universal practice among the large corporations supporting educational programs outside their own jurisdiction. Plans differ in the extent of the financial help offered, the particular courses approved, and the employees eligible for assistance. Financial help varies anywhere from 40 per cent up to the full amount of the tuition, with differing policies

[6] *The College Blue Book,* 8th ed., Christian E. Burckel, Editor and Publisher, Yonkers, N.Y., 1956, pp. 233–248.

regarding travel, laboratory fees, and books. Some companies place an over-all limit of from $120 to $200 on the educational expenditures of any one student during any calendar year. Assistance is invariably contingent upon a passing grade and is not infrequently arranged according to a sliding scale, depending upon the grade received. It is generally required that the institution be fully accredited, and that the course be relevant to the employee's present position or one in prospect. Leniency is often exercised in this latter requirement, as for instance where a student employee is a candidate for a degree, and required courses are stipulated by the college or university. Occasionally, a company permits any course that increases one's knowledge and understanding of the world. Tuition rebates are generally open to all full-time employees of a year or more standing; sometimes they are open to all, regardless of the term of employment. Although tuition refund plans usually apply to after-hours courses, in nearby institutions, it is not uncommon for those in upper managerial categories to be granted a leave of absence for extended study in some more distant university. Such accommodation is usually contingent upon a stipulated term of employment with the company and a record of interest in higher education manifested by successful completion of courses of study on a college level. If salary is reduced or withheld during the leave of absence, a more liberal share of tuition expenses is frequently assumed by the company.

Education Below the College Level

Plans for employee assistance in formal educational institutions below the college level follow much the same patterns as those for help in institutions of higher learning. They are not, however, so generally available, many companies restricting such assistance to the more advanced levels. In Chapter VIII attention was called to a company program in general education offering high-school courses for which a diploma, fully accredited by the local and state boards of education, might be earned, but this plan is a novelty rather than one representative of a pattern. It may not be very different from an accredited evening high-school program.

The Work Experience Education Program on a high-school level is the counterpart of the co-operative plan for engineering students explained above. It was introduced shortly after the Cincinnati plan was inaugurated, appropriately, in the Cincinnati public schools. By 1928 approximately 5,682 pupils were enrolled in co-operative courses in 78 cities scattered throughout the country; by 1954–1955 the number had increased to 24,236.

The plan provides for the co-ordination of employment with classroom instruction, and time spent at work is regarded as time spent in school. Students usually attend classes in the morning and report for work in the afternoon. They are paid at current wage rates and conform, of course, to all local, state, and federal youth-employment regulations. A teacher co-ordinator acts as liaison between industry and the school system, and the pupil's final grade is a composite of his or her work record and class performance.[7]

One company has a thoroughly organized routine for employing boys following such work-study programs when approved by local school authorities.[8] This program offers selected seniors in high schools and students in technical schools the same on-the-job instruction as is given to new employees. Teaching is conducted by department managers, job instructors, or other experienced personnel selected by the manager. Students rotate through various job assignments according to their choice of programs. A student may choose an assignment in the production department where he will learn machine-tool operations and inspection methods, or in secretarial and office practice where experience may be gained in filing, typing, dictation, transcription, and general office practices. Technical institute students can be assigned to departments appropriate to their major interests— mechanical, electrical, or chemical, as the case may be. The usual work week for high-school students is 4 hours a day, 5 days a week; for those attending technical schools, it depends upon the school program. Upon completion of each work assignment, the

[7] *Work Experience Education Programs, op. cit.*

[8] Information furnished through the courtesy of the International Business Machines Corporation, New York.

department manager submits a written evaluation of the student's performance, and upon termination of the entire rotation, the school authorities are advised of the student's record in order that proper credit may be given. Some of these work-study programs are still in the experimental stage, especially those designed primarily to reduce the number of students discontinuing school when the legally prescribed age has been reached. For selected students, however, the plan seems to have worked successfully, providing a rare opportunity for those who could not otherwise afford to continue their education, as well as for others who may wish to gain work experience to assist them in making a decision as to a life career.

Tuition refund plans are frequently, although not always, applied indiscriminately to college-level courses and those of a more elementary nature. On the nondegree level, practices differ most widely in appraising correspondence courses. In some instances such courses are encouraged; in others they are excluded. Some companies permit them only when no formal classes are available; others pass upon each individual application separately.

Scholarships, Fellowships, and Loans

Although not included in the questionnaire on which this study is based, no account of the educational activities conducted by American industry would be complete without reference to the liberal scholarship funds often granted by corporations to their employees and to the families of employees.

One company provides annually 40 scholarship awards of $600 each for the sons and daughters of its employees. Any one recipient may receive four such awards, making possible continued assistance during the 4 years of college. In addition, a direct grant of $500 is made to each accredited privately controlled college or university attended by a scholarship recipient.[9] Another company awards scholarships covering the full cost of tuition up to a maximum of $700, in addition to a stipend amounting to two-thirds of the expenses for room and board, not exceeding

[9] The Ohio Oil Company, Findlay, Ohio, *Scholarship Plan Providing College Scholarship Benefits for Children of Employees,* a brochure.

$500.[10] A third plan offers scholarships to the sons of employees on a competitive basis, in amounts varying according to salaries received. For the sons of employees earning up to $7,000 a year, the scholarship provides full payment of all tuition fees, board, room, books, supplies, miscellaneous living expenses, and transportation to and from the college each semester. For the sons of employees receiving from $7,000 to $15,000 a year, the amount varies, depending upon circumstances.[11] It is not uncommon for a corporation offering a work-study plan for technical students to include a scholarship covering at least part of the tuition.

Finally, educational loan funds are sometimes provided for employees and their children. In one case the loans are made at no interest and are repayable in easy stages over a period of years after schooling is complete.[12]

[10] Weyerhaeuser Timber Foundation (financed largely by contributions from the Weyerhaeuser Timber Company, Tacoma, Wash.), *Scholarship Program to Provide College or University Scholarships for the Sons and Daughters of Weyerhaeuser Employees,* a brochure.

[11] U.S. Industries, Inc., New York, *Scholarship Program for the Sons of Employees,* a brochure.

[12] Burlington Industries, Incorporated, Greensboro, N.C., *Thirty Years of the Burlington Story,* a brochure, p. 39.

The famous Horatio Alger, Jr., it is said, sold upward of 20,000,000 books during the latter part of the nineteenth century, all based on the single theme of rags to riches by way of frugality, industry, and fortuitous events. A modern success story could well be placed in the setting of a big corporation. But whatever might be said about industry and frugality, fortuitous events need not be invoked, because today the corporations offer an abundance of opportunities. If willing, able, and fortunate enough to find employment in the right companies at the strategic time, our hero can start with scant education. He can attend high school, complete college, and go on to a master's degree, even a doctorate, all under the watchful eye of the corporation, counseled and encouraged all the way. He will receive compensation and, no doubt, some aid toward his expenses. The final reward will not be a business of his own, for this modern hero probably does not want one. What he wants, more likely, is a managerial post in some big corporation, and, given the innate ability and disposition to learn, he will probably get it.

It would be hard to find, in recent years, a more thoroughgoing shift in values than that manifested by industry's preoccupation with education. Certainly in Alger's day the college graduate, entering business, was received with open doubt, tinged with disdain, which could be mitigated only by quickly laying aside his learning and acquiring the ways of practical men. Today, not only is the learning essential, but it must be augmented throughout life. Spurred by necessity, the change has been instigated by industry, with significant effects upon formal education, and not without overtones for American culture as a whole.

Specialization beyond the compass of universities and technical schools has forced industry to provide systematic graduate instruction in specific areas; the highly technical nature of advanced research has prompted co-operative work-study programs, enabling personnel to continue their education toward second and third degrees; and rapid technological progress makes it essential that employees keep abreast of new ideas, processes, and inventions. Changing production techniques, with automation and nuclear energy already on the horizon, require upgrading and constant retraining on a large scale; and man-power shortage has prompted industry to search even secondary-school levels for talent that can be trained in various assistant capacities, often while formal education is continued. And these activities have only just begun. As the American people demand more and more products of a technical nature, competent personnel must be trained in prodigious numbers for research, production, marketing, and service activities, with a large share of the burden falling upon industry.

No less urgent has been the training necessitated by the constantly increasing professionalization of management. The many programs, designed for the benefit of selected graduates slated for responsible posts, bear witness to the fact that college education is not enough. Demands on managerial skill and knowledge have multiplied to such an extent during the twentieth century that the liberal-arts graduate must have specialized knowledge of the principles and methods involved; the technical graduate, aspiring to a managerial post, must have a broad background in liberal education to enable him to cope with the wide variety of decisions that he will be called upon to make, and both need to supplement college learning with systematic instruction and guidance while acquiring experience.

Evolution of the factory from an overgrown workshop to a major social institution has prompted industry to cull the social sciences for better methods of dealing with people. The importance of attitudes, the danger of frustration, ways of providing motivation and assuring job satisfaction, the significance of group loyalties, the art of communicating in such a way as to impart understanding and gain acceptance, factors that make for leadership—these and many other concepts have been codified into courses of instruction essential for supervisory personnel.

Even top management has found it necessary to go back to school. Combining in associations of their own creation, participating in courses offered by many colleges and universities, and attending corporation seminars, they keep informed of current ideas and acquire new techniques applicable to their particular interests.

As a consequence of these varied and extensive educational activities organized by leading corporations, new trends are discernible in American education as a whole. Certainly the fact that an academic degree is now a near prerequisite to a successful career in a big corporation has something to do with mounting college enrollments, far exceeding anything attributable to an increasing population. But the statistics for college enrollments alone are somewhat misleading if viewed in the light of the custom of spending four rather leisurely years on a college campus, with at least three summers of vacation, or perhaps vacation combined with some not too arduous remunerative activity. The United States Census reports that in October, 1956, 800,000 college students were employed part or full time, or nearly 30 per cent of the total enrollment, more than in any year since World War II.[1] This, in itself, might indicate a trend away from the traditional 4 years occupied exclusively with studies.

But other considerations must be taken into account. There is a difference between a full-time student with a part-time job and a part-time student with a full-time job. The census figures would seem to include both. Part-time students alone numbered something over 500,000 in 1955, or $22\frac{1}{2}$ per cent of the total enrollment for that year. The increase of part-time students for the period from 1953 to 1955 accounts, in fact, for over a quarter of the total

[1] *Facts on File 1956,* Weekly World News Digest, Inc., New York, pp. 30, A3; 23, A3.

increased college enrollment during that period.[2] A full-time
student with a part-time job suggests an emphasis upon income
without much notice as to how it is obtained. This is understandable, since college expenses have almost doubled since 1939–1940.[3]
No doubt the income incentive is a factor with the part-time
student also, but here the emphasis is usually upon the job, suggesting an integration of work and study rarely possible with the
full-time student.

Supplementing work with related study is the very thing being
encouraged by industry. It would seem, therefore, that this policy
on the part of industry is responsible in large measure for the
increase in numbers and percentages of part-time students, and
the resulting change in the climate of many a college campus.
Credence is given this interpretation by the fact that there is a
significant correlation between highly industrialized regions and
the number of part-time students attending institutions of higher
learning within those regions. Such figures are available by states,
the coefficient of correlation being 0.86. And, as might be expected,
there is a significant correlation between states highly urbanized
and the number of part-time students within those states. The
coefficient of correlation in this case is 0.62.[4] Evidently industry's
insistence upon education is being felt, for the most part, by urban
institutions in highly industrialized areas.

Whether or not this trend is desirable for American culture as
a whole is a moot question. Some claim that a part-time student
suffers a disadvantage in selecting the courses that he wants and

[2] *Resident and Extension Enrollment in Institutions of Higher Education,*
Circular 493, U.S. Department of Health, Education, and Welfare, Washington, D.C., November, 1955. These figures are conservative, since a part-
time student is defined as one taking 75 per cent of the number of credit
hours required for graduation divided by the number of semesters normally
taken for graduation. Students enrolled in the co-operative plan, explained
in Chapter IX, would not be classified as part-time students according to
this definition.

[3] *Facts on File 1957,* Weekly World News Digest, Inc., New York, p. 151,
D1.

[4] *Resident and Extension Enrollment in Institutions of Higher Education,*
op. cit.; and *Portfolio of United States Census Maps,* U.S. Department of
Commerce, Bureau of the Census, Washington, D.C., 1950.

should take, because of restrictions on his time schedule. He is therefore inclined, it is said, to enroll in almost any course that is available and permitted by the regulations, as long as it counts toward a degree.[5] Of course, if the college curriculum is designed exclusively for full-time study, this may be true. But is there any compelling reason why a college curriculum should be so designed? A period of rapid change is at hand for education as well as for industry. To be sure, an institution of learning, adhering to traditional ways, can probably survive longer than a commercial institution pursuing a like policy, but, as time goes on, even this tenure of existence becomes precarious. On the other hand, the necessary adjustment would not seem to be insurmountable. Certainly many institutions of unquestioned standing have succeeded in accomplishing it, apparently without undue dislocations.

The impact of industrial educational activities on the secondary-school level is not so clearly defined. It is manifested more in potential possibilities than in present actualities. The most promising area at the moment seems to be in the work-experience-education movement explained elsewhere in this report.[6] It is estimated that in 1956 about 45 per cent of high-school students discontinued their studies before graduation. This is a material improvement over the 60 per cent in 1946,[7] but it is still far too high in an age when an adequate education means so much. Organized community efforts, largely in the nature of persuasion, are being brought to bear on the problem,[8] but it is an open question whether this approach is sufficient. Motivation seems to be lacking. Young people, who dislike schoolwork and impatiently await the legal minimum age when they can get a permanent job, are not particularly impressed with arguments pic-

[5] John W. Dykstra, "I Worked My Way Through College," *Phi Delta Kappan,* Vol. XXXVIII, No. 9, June, 1957, p. 379.

[6] See p. 124.

[7] *Facts on File 1956,* Weekly World News Digest, Inc., New York, p. 295, G1.

[8] *National Stay-In-School Campaign, Handbook for Communities,* U.S. Department of Health, Education, and Welfare, Office of Education, Washington, D.C.

turing regrets sometime in the indefinite future over opportunities shunned today.

Once placed in the environment of a modern industrial establishment, however, it is hard to see how the most recalcitrant youth can fail to be impressed with the need for education. Thus motivated, and, assuming the necessary mental capacity, his interest in schoolwork might well take a turn for the better. As already noted, some progressive companies have made systematic provision for employing youth during released school time, thus lending impetus to the movement in certain areas. In other localities the plan has been instigated by the school authorities, with industry co-operating.[9] The very fact that more than 1,500,000 high-school students are gainfully employed[10] would go to show that there is a demand for their services, and, on the part of many, a willingness to work. It remains to capitalize these opportunities in the form of a greater number of integrated work-study programs spread over a larger area. The incentive to do so may well be intensified as more of the smaller companies follow the lead of the big corporations in establishing appropriate educational programs.

That the formal institutions of higher learning, and to a lesser extent those on a secondary level, should be the first to feel the impact of industry's educational activities is to be expected. Even in this immediate area, however, it is too soon fully to evaluate the consequences. To suggest more general social effects is still more speculative. At the same time, certain changes can be discerned which are sufficiently related to this new sector being added to American education to deserve mention.

There can no longer be much doubt that forces of some kind are at work increasing occupational mobility. This is not to say that the day is at hand when equal opportunity for all in attaining complete fulfillment of whatever innate capacity may exist.

[9] *Work Experience Education Programs, American Secondary Schools,* Bulletin No. 5, U.S. Department of Health, Education, and Welfare, Office of Education, Washington, D.C., 1957.

[10] *Facts on File 1956,* Weekly World News Digest, Inc., New York, p. 39, A3.

Financial position, influential connection, accidents of birth, even fortuitous events still bulk large in life's scramble for success. But, considered in the perspective of time, opportunities are becoming less restricted.

In 1928 an exhaustive study of the social origins of business leaders was made by two outstanding scholars.[11] A recent and equally authoritative study, using the same methods and techniques, presents comparable data for 1952. The results show that the sons of business and professional men were less likely to become business leaders in 1952 than in 1928, while the sons of laborers, farmers, and white-collar workers were more likely to attain such levels in the latter than in the former year, both by a considerable margin.[12] It seems a reasonable inference that education has exerted a considerable influence in this change. As already pointed out, it was the period between the two wars when events conspired to direct the attention of industry to the advantages of formally trained personnel, and, although the intensive educational drive within industry did not get started until later, it then served to widen the already increasing educational opportunities characteristic of the period. It seems reasonable to believe that the intensified emphasis upon education and the increased opportunities to attain it, both owing to industry in some measure, at least helped shift the weight of advantage from social privilege to intellectual competence.

One corporation has observed that industry, cognizant of its social power, has felt the need of increased emphasis upon education.[13] Is it not probable that education, in turn, has exerted some influence upon the direction in which that power is exercised?

Management has, during the past half century, been divested first of ownership, then control, of the corporate structure, and has been left with the sole function of assuming the multitudinous

[11] F. W. Taussig and C. S. Joslyn, *American Business Leaders,* The Macmillan Company, New York, 1932.

[12] W. Lloyd Warner and James C. Abegglen, *Big Business Leaders in America,* Harper & Brothers, New York, 1955, p. 17.

[13] International Harvester Company, *Adult Education in Industry,* a brochure, undated.

responsibilities of operating vast industrial enterprises.[14] And these responsibilities have increased materially during the period cited. The day of intuitive decisions, crude methods, and dominance of forceful, if sometimes arbitrary, personalities has passed. Instead, certain knowledge, recognized skills, and an ability to inspire co-operative effort are required. Education has been the means to these ends and is now recognized as a continuous adjunct to experience.

Effective education engenders change. It is not surprising, therefore, that striking changes have occurred in numerous relationships between industry and the rest of society during recent years. Regard for community welfare in business decisions, amenability to public opinion, support of philanthropic and educational institutions, and contributions to the stabilization of world economic affairs are cases in point.[15]

Two great educational innovations of an institutional nature have shaped the civilization in which we live. The first had its beginning back in the latter part of the thirteenth century when groups of teachers or scholars, or both, banded together in the form of medieval guilds to secure mutual protection and unmolested seclusion in the pursuit of knowledge. Thus were inaugurated the first permanent organizations for the transmission of learning. The second was the establishment of the American free public-school system, accomplished, in principle at least, by the close of the second quarter of the nineteenth century. From the first has evolved the modern university; from the second, the conception of universal education, supported by the people and free from both the taint of charity and the influence of selfish interests.

It is possible that we are now witnessing, in the educational activities of American industry, the birth of a third great educational force of far-reaching consequences.[16] For, just as the first

[14] Peter Drucker, *America's Next Twenty Years*, reprint from the March, April, May, and June, 1955, issues of *Harper's Magazine*.

[15] A. A. Berle, Jr., *The Twentieth Century Capitalist Revolution*, Harcourt, Brace and Company, Inc., New York, 1954, Chap. V.

[16] Eugene Staley (Ed.), *Creating an Industrial Civilization, a Report on the Corning Conference*, Harper & Brothers, New York, 1952, p. 48.

has perpetuated learning, and the second has provided the bulwarks for democracy and for a free economy, so this third innovation is adapting civilization to a new technological era, the ultimate consequences of which stagger the imagination. Nor is this merely an adjustment to mechanical wonders. It is an integration of new technical skills with revitalized human relationships, envisaging a world augmented not only in material comforts but, far more important, in spiritual values.

Bibliography

Allen, Frederick Lewis, *The Big Change, America Transforms Itself,* Harper & Brothers, New York, 1952.

Apprenticeship Past and Present, 3rd ed., U.S. Department of Labor, Bureau of Apprenticeship, Washington, D.C., 1955.

Beatty, A. J., *Corporation Schools,* Public School Publishing Company, Bloomington, Ill., 1918.

Bendix, Reinhard, *Work and Authority in Industry, Ideologies of Management in the Course of Industrialization,* John Wiley & Sons, Inc., New York, 1956.

Berle, A. A., Jr., *The Twentieth Century Capitalist Revolution,* Harcourt, Brace and Company, Inc., New York, 1954.

Berle, Adolf A., Jr., and Means, Gardner C., *The Modern Corporation and Private Property,* The Macmillan Company, New York, 1933.

Bursk, Edward C. (Ed.), *Human Relations for Management, the Newer Perspective,* Harper & Brothers, New York, 1956.

Business Week, McGraw-Hill Publishing Company, Inc., New York, p. 64, Aug. 18, 1956.

Chapman, Gilbert W., "Educating Tomorrow's Executives," *The Management Review,* American Management Association, New York, p. 78, March, 1957.

Classified Index of Occupations and Industries of 1950 Census of Population, U.S. Department of Commerce, Bureau of the Census, Washington, D.C., 1950.

College Blue Book, The, 8th ed., Christian E. Burkel, Editor and Publisher, Yonkers, N. Y., 1956.

Diamond, Sigmund, *The Reputation of the American Businessman,* Harvard University Press, Cambridge, Mass., 1955.

Diebold, John, *Automation, the Advent of the Automatic Factory,* D. Van Nostrand Company, Inc., New York, 1952.

Drucker, Peter, *America's Next Twenty Years,* reprint from the March, April, May, and June, 1955, issues of *Harper's Magazine.*

Dykstra, John W., "I Worked My Way Through College," *Phi Delta Kappan,* Vol. XXXVIII, No. 9, June, 1957.

Eells, Richard, *Corporation Giving in a Free Society,* Harper & Brothers, New York, 1956.

Einzig, Paul, *The Economic Consequences of Automation,* W. W. Norton & Company, Inc., New York, 1956.

Encyclopedia of the Social Sciences, The, The Macmillan Company, New York, 1930.

Executive Life, The, The Editors of Fortune, Doubleday & Company, Inc., New York, 1956.

Facts on File 1956 and *1957,* Weekly World News Digest, Inc., New York.

Fisher, Burton R., and Withey, Stephen H., *Big Business as the People See It,* The Survey Research Center, University of Michigan, Ann Arbor, Mich., 1951.

Friedmann, Georges, *Industrial Society,* Free Press, Glencoe, Ill., 1955.

Fryer, Douglas H., Feinberg, Mortimer R., and Zalkind, Sheldon S., *Developing People in Industry,* Harper & Brothers, New York, 1946.

Haire, Mason, *Psychology in Management,* McGraw-Hill Book Company, Inc., New York, 1956.

Handbook of Basic Economic Statistics, Economic Statistics Bureau of Washington, D.C., January, 1957.

Highlights for the Executive, Studies in Personnel Policy No. 160, National Industrial Conference Board, New York.

Hugh-Jones, E. M. (Ed.), *The Push-Button World, Automation Today,* University of Oklahoma Press, Norman, Okla., 1956.

Instrumentation and Automation, Hearings Before the Subcommittee on Economic Stabilization of the Joint Economic Committee, Congress of the United States, Second Session, Dec. 12, 13, and 14, 1956, U.S. Government Printing Office, Washington, D.C., 1957.

Lauterbach, Albert, *Man, Motives, and Money, Psychological Frontiers of Economics,* Cornell University Press, Ithaca, N. Y., 1954.

Maier, Norman R. F., *Principles of Human Relations,* John Wiley & Sons, Inc., New York, 1952.

Management Education for Itself and Its Employees, Parts I to IV, American Management Association, New York, 1954.

Mighty Force of Research, The, The Editors of Fortune, McGraw-Hill Book Company, Inc., New York, 1956.

Moulton, Harold, *Income and Economic Progress,* Brookings Institution, Washington, D.C., 1935.

National Stay-in-School Campaign, Handbook for Communities, U.S. Department of Health, Education, and Welfare, Office of Education, Washington, D.C.

Newcomer, Mabel, *The Big Business Executive, the Factors That Made Him,* Columbia University Press, New York, 1955.

Osborn, Alex F., *Applied Imagination, Principles and Practices of Creative Thinking,* rev. ed., Charles Scribner's Sons, New York, 1957.

Patterson, William, and Hedges, Marion, *Educating for Industry Through Apprenticeship,* Prentice-Hall, Inc., Englewood Cliffs, N.J., 1947.

Personnel, American Management Association, New York, March, 1953.

Portfolio of United States Census Maps, U.S. Department of Commerce, Bureau of the Census, Washington, D.C., 1950.

Resident and Extension Enrollment in Institutions of Higher Education, Circular 493, U.S. Department of Health, Education, and Welfare, Washington, D.C., November, 1955.

Scholarships and Fellowships Available at Institutions of Higher Education, Bulletin No. 16, Federal Security Agency, Office of Education, Washington, D.C., 1951.

Sloan, Harold S., "The Educational Backgrounds of Business Leaders in the United States," *Challenge Magazine,* Institute of Economic Affairs, New York University, New York, December, 1953.

Smith, Henry Clay, *Psychology of Industrial Behavior,* McGraw-Hill Book Company, Inc., New York, 1955.

Special Report No. 44, National Policy Association, Washington, D.C., 1956.

Staley, Eugene (Ed.), *Creating an Industrial Civilization, a Report on the Corning Conference,* Harper & Brothers, New York, 1952.

Statistical Abstract of the United States, 77th ann. ed., U.S. Department of Commerce, Washington, D.C., 1956.

Studies in Personnel Policy No. 107, National Industrial Conference Board, New York, 1950.

Taussig, F. W., and Joslyn, C. S., *American Business Leaders,* The Macmillan Company, New York, 1932.

U.S. Commissioner of Labor, *17th Annual Report,* Washington, D.C., 1902.

Warner, W. Lloyd, and Abegglen, James C., *Big Business Leaders in America,* Harper & Brothers, New York, 1955.

Warner, W. Lloyd, and Abegglen, James C., *Occupational Mobility in American Business and Industry, 1928-1952,* University of Minnesota Press, Minneapolis, 1955.

Whyte, William H., Jr., *The Organization Man,* Simon and Schuster, Inc., New York, 1956.

Work Experience Education Programs, American Secondary Schools, Bulletin No. 5, U.S. Department of Health, Education, and Welfare, Office of Education, Washington, D.C., 1957.